A Gathering of Eagles

Scenes from
Roman Scotland

Gordon Maxwell

Series editor: Gordon Barclay

BIRLINN LTD
with

HISTORIC SCOTLAND

THE MAKING OF SCOTLAND

Titles Available

WILD HARVESTERS: The First People in Scotland

FARMERS, TEMPLES AND TOMBS:
Scotland in the Neolithic and Early Bronze Age

SETTLEMENT AND SACRIFICE:
The Later Prehistoric People of Scotland

A GATHERING OF EAGLES: Scenes from Roman Scotland

SURVIVING IN SYMBOLS: A Visit to the Pictish Nation

SAINTS AND SEA-KINGS: The First Kingdom of the Scots

ANGELS, FOOLS AND TYRANTS: Britons and Anglo-Saxons
in Southern Scotland (AD 450–750)

THE SEA ROAD: A Viking Voyage through Scotland

ALBA: The Gaelic Kingdom of Scotland AD 800–1124

BURGESS, MERCHANT AND PRIEST: Burgh Life in
The Scottish Medieval Town

PUIR LABOURERS AND BUSY HUSBANDMEN:
The Countryside of Lowland Scotland in the Middle Ages

THE AGE OF THE CLANS:
The Highlands from Somerled to the Clearances

First published in 1998 by Canongate Books Ltd.
This edition published in 2005 by Birlinn Ltd,
10 Newington Road, Edinburgh EH9 1QS

www.birlinn.co.uk

ISBN 1 84158 384 7

Series Design: James Hutcheson

Design: Janet Watson

Printed and bound by GraphyCems

Previous page
A Monument for Posterity
The Antonine Wall at Watling Lodge, near Falkirk
HISTORIC SCOTLAND

A GATHERING
OF EAGLES

Contents

Prologue   7

Forced Entry: Invasion and Conquest   15

The Sinews of Power   27

Occupation   37

Epilogue   50

How Do I Find Out More?   59

Further Reading   63

Acknowledgements   64

Trajan's Column
The Roman army at the start of the second century.
ANGUS LAMB

'Eight eagles were then seen, which flew off into the woods,
a splendid omen. . . "After them", shouted Germanicus, "they are the
Legions' guardian spirits.'"
Tacitus, *Annals*, II, 17.

'The chief standard of the entire legion is the eagle,
carried by the eagle-bearer.'
Flavius Vegetius Renatus, *Epitome of Military Science,* II, 13.

'If, however, it is put into italics, in a conversational form, separate
from the actual scholarship, then the hypothesis remains only a
hypothesis and doesn't undermine the seriousness of the work.'
Umberto Eco, *Foucault's Pendulum*.

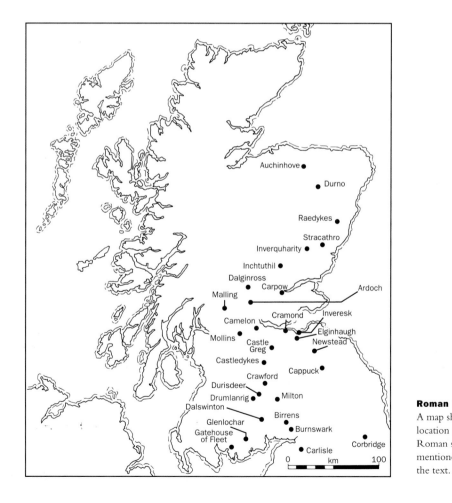

Roman Scotland
A map showing the
location of the main
Roman sites
mentioned in
the text.

Prologue

The year is AD 383, and the Spaniard Magnus Maximus, newly appointed to a senior command in the five-province Diocese of Britannia, has been persuaded to make a bid for control of the Western Empire, challenging the two sons of the emperor Valentinian I, Gratian and Valentinian the younger, and hoping to become the colleague of his former comrade-in-arms and distant kinsman, the Eastern Emperor Theodosius the Great. From York, the capital of the northernmost province of the Diocese, he writes a letter to an old friend. . .

MAGNUS MAXIMUS, DUX
BRITANNIARUM, JUSTINIANO
FRATRI SUO AC CONTUBERNALI
ANTIQUO PLURIMAM SALUTEM.

scr. Eboraco xii Kal. Apr., Gratiano Augusto et
Merobaude conss.

Ridiculosior sane tibi viderer, frater, si me ad
scrinia mea nunc deprehenderes. . .

To Justinianus, his old messmate, Magnus
Maximus, Duke of the Five Provinces of
Britain, sends his warmest greetings!

Governor's Lodge

York

21st March

You really would smile to see me now, sitting
at a desk piled high with obsolete military
intelligence: dusty maps, dog-eared plans of
forts, reports of long-dead Governors of the
Five Provinces of Britannia; rosters of regiments
that no longer exist. Rarefied reading for this
time of night! Yet for several days now I have
been engrossed by my task, a night-owl
picking over the bones of the Eagles; and
you would not smile to learn the reason
for my labours.

Britannia is in excellent
shape, but across the Channel, as you will have heard, things are in a poor state. Germany is overflowing with her pernicious brood: Frankish invasions today, Vandals, Alans, and Suevi tomorrow. Not that we in this island have lacked troubles of our own, but a firm hand can work wonders. It was much worse sixteen years ago, when we also had to deal with internal treachery. Picts and Scots are never slow to sniff out any weakness, and could not fail to notice the destabilising effect of all the civil unrest under Constantius, but when our own men, our eyes and ears beyond the frontier Wall, were bribed to act as double agents, the situation became hopeless. What a stroke of luck that Valentinian eventually decided to send out the elder Theodosius with his field-army!

The point of all this reminiscing is two-fold: first, to confirm that the secret of ensuring peace and prosperity in Britannia is to maintain an effective northern military command, both by having well-trained, well-equipped troops in the right places, and by keeping our ears close to the ground on both sides of the Frontier Wall; and secondly, and more

Magnus Maximus
'You really would smile to see me now. Sitting at a desk
piled high with obsolete military intelligence…'
CHRIS BROWN

importantly, to realise that, although Theodosius is a thoroughly reliable Emperor, his sphere of action lies beyond the Adriatic, while the entire Western Empire must risk ruin under the feckless sons of Valentinian.

You'll have guessed where all this is leading, the more so because it is something you have always encouraged me to do. Well, yesterday, I finally acceded to the requests of the Legions; within a day or two I shall be acclaimed as emperor by the Diocesan Council in Augusta [London]. I not only invite you to join with me now in this venture, I also want you to help me determine how the next phase must be managed: namely, how Britannia is to be kept safe while you and I, and a sizeable part of the British garrison, risk our lives on the far side of the Channel. From intelligence reports, it seems unlikely that the Prefecture of the Gauls will present much opposition to our move, although the barbarian levies might make a token stand. I will not, therefore, need to strip the frontier of its guards. Nevertheless,

something must be done to bind the people of the north more firmly to us, and somehow we shall have to make sure that the garrisons we leave behind understand our tactical and strategic objectives in that quarter.

That is why I have ransacked the provincial archives here in York, and why I am asking you to come directly here while I play politics in London. What you must do is to go through these documents, omitting nothing, and get an overview of the entire course of frontier history. Examine the successes and failures of our dealings with the north, and assess the effectiveness of our modern, and past, garrisons and installations. Incidentally, a fellow-Spaniard, Vegetius Renatus, showed me the material he was collecting for a publication on just this subject. It's a pity his work isn't yet complete; you would have found it useful.

In the meantime, have fun with the files. I'm off to gather in the Eagles.

Farewell!

A Legionary Eagle
Britannia places a tiny wreath in the beak of the eagle-image crowning the Twentieth Legion standard. From a second-century carved stone found near Bearsden. HUNTERIAN MUSEUM, UNIVERSITY OF GLASGOW

Within a fortnight, Maximus receives the following reply:

To His Imperial Highness Magnus Maximus, Justinianus, Commander of Frontier Forces, Britannia, sends greeting!

Governor's Lodge
York
2nd April

Well, I've done all that you asked, to the best of my ability. Taking you at your word, I've concentrated on the north, but omitted nothing, even though the files go back to the expeditions of the late Republic. (Knowing your weak grasp of history, I've added the consular dates, where necessary, and provided notes about the strength and organisation of the province's early garrison.)

Julius Caesar was the first Roman actually to land an army on these shores [in 55 and 54 BC], and several of the early emperors had plans for Britain: Augustus thought about invading it on several occasions [between 34 BC and AD 7], and Caligula aborted an invasion at the last moment [AD 40], but the island did not become part of the Empire until Claudius personally oversaw its conquest [in AD 43]. These plans were all preoccupied with the south-east corner of the island, and with the usual confused mass of pretexts and objectives – the political glory conferred by a victory won beyond the narrow strip of Ocean, the military need to destroy a possible refuge for our enemies, and, of course, the diplomatic claims that numerous British refugees have had on our protection.

Once begun in earnest, the conquest proceeded in a series of waves. In the reigns of Claudius and Nero [i.e. until AD 68], we secured our grip on the south-eastern lowlands and began to address the problems of controlling the western and northern uplands. After Nero's removal [in AD 68], the successive emperors of the Flavian dynasty presided over the most extensive annexation of British territory since the original invasion. Under Vespasian all the land west of the River Severn and northwards as far as the fringes of Caledonia was either overrun or occupied, first of all when Petillius Cerealis was governor, then by his successor, Julius Frontinus (who wrote several of the memoranda I've been reading), and latterly by Julius Agricola. When Vespasian died [AD 79], his elder son, Titus, re-appointed Agricola with orders to consolidate everything south of the isthmus between Forth and Clyde. However, Titus' brother, Domitian [succeeded AD 81], soon had him advancing through Caledonia again, and within two years Agricola had fought the northern tribes to a standstill at the battle of *Mons Graupius.* If it hadn't been for the troubles on the Danube, which resulted in the need to cut back on manpower (some things never change!), Agricola's successor might have led the legions to the very furthest tip of the island. As it was, the files of this period record nothing but retrenchment – first of all withdrawal from territory north of the Forth [by AD 87], and then, about twelve years later, humiliating retreat to a line between Tyne and Solway, at which time Trajan was on the throne. Not surprisingly, there's a lot of information available for the Flavian period, due in part to the fact that Agricola's son-in-law (and biographer) was the historian Cornelius Tacitus. Considering this relationship, I'm not sure we should trust everything he says!

The following years are much more sparsely covered: innumerable folders of administrative papers – unit-strength returns and the like, but few detailed situation reports. It's almost as if there had been a complete reversal of strategy: from the open, fluid frontier-zones of the Flavians, to the fixed, continuous barrier which is still with us today. At first this barrier was the wall of Hadrian, constructed between Tyne and Solway at the lowest ebb of Flavian retreat [begun AD 122]; then 20 years later, a replacement wall, this time

ROMAN ARMY ORGANISATION – FROM THE FLAVIAN TO SEVERAN PERIOD				
Unit/CO	Status/Average number in Britain	Sub-units/ officers	Total manpower per unit	Ranker's pay (in *denarii*)
Legion/ Praetorian Legate	Roman citizen (elite)/ 4 until AD 86/7, 3 thereafter	Nine 6-century (500 man) cohorts + one double cohort of infantry, under centurions + c. 120 cavalry	c. 5500 per legion	300 (infantry) 400 (cavalry)
Auxiliaries	Mostly non-Roman (second line troops)			
Quingenary infantry cohort/Prefect	c. 18	Six 80-man centuries, each of ten (8-man) *contubernia*, under centurions	c. 500	100
Milliary infantry cohort / Tribune	2	Ten 80-man centuries each of ten (8-man) *contubernia* under centurions	c. 800	100
Quingenary cavalry *ala* / Prefect	c. 15	Sixteen 30-man troops, under decurions	c. 500	333
Milliary cavalry *ala* / Tribune	1	Twenty-four 30-man troops, under decurions	c. 750	333
Quingenary equitate cohort / Prefect	c. 30	Four 30-man troops of cavalry, under decurions + six 60-man centuries of infantry, under centurions	c. 500	100 (infantry) 200 (cavalry)
Milliary equitate cohort / Prefect	c. 5	Eight 30-man troops, under decurions + ten c. 70-man centuries, under centurions	c. 1000	100 (infantry) 200 (cavalry)

A member of the Roman re-enactment group The Antonine Guard.
THE ANTONINE GUARD

Note: The numbers of auxiliary garrisons varied over time and are approximate.

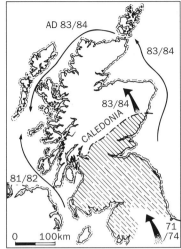

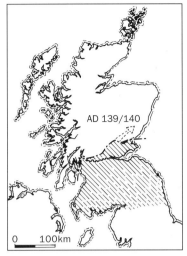

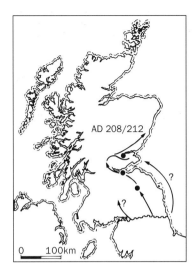

Third Century

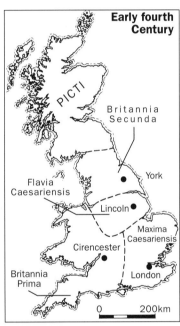

Early fourth Century

Late fourth Century

Conquest, Occupation and Administration
Military activity in Roman Scotland in the Flavian, Antonine and Severan periods, together with later provincial sub-divisions of the Diocese of Britannia, as well as later capitals.

Bronze Visor Mask
A visor mask from the fort at Newstead, near Melrose, which would have been worn by a member of a well-paid cavalry unit.
NATIONAL MUSEUMS OF SCOTLAND

of turf, was built between Forth and Clyde, on the orders of the emperor Antoninus Pius – a project which necessitated re-occupation of much of what had been conquered in Flavian times. Although in some ways less ambitious, this Antonine frontier lasted much longer than its predecessors, and cost less to build and maintain, despite some hefty repair bills in its middle years, than the wall of Hadrian. Nevertheless, about two years into the reign of Marcus Aurelius [say around AD 163], after only two decades of productive life, the Antonine Wall was abandoned, leaving only a handful of outpost forts to maintain a Roman presence north of the recommissioned Hadrianic wall.

The files of the next 40 years are either hopelessly jumbled or tantalisingly nibbled by mice. Yet it is clear that the unsupervised northern tribes had become a menace, constantly threatening to break through the frontier defences. They succeeded at least twice in this period, first under Commodus [around AD 184], and again in the early years of the emperor Septimius Severus [between AD 197 and 200].

These Severan campaigns [AD 208-211] were the last real attempt to take a full Roman army into the heart of barbarian territory; most of what came later was an extended field-exercise, when all we risked was having our pockets picked by the locals. However, it was more than pilfering that Severus was up against when he came to Britain. To begin with, there was the awkwardness of a previous governor, Clodius Albinus, who had decided [AD 193] to attempt to win the imperial throne, and had taken a sizeable detachment across to Gaul to fight for him. When he was killed, our 'friends in the north', with whom he seems to have had an 'agreement', decided that his death had cancelled all debts, and they began to overwhelm elements of the reduced frontier force. Virius Lupus, Albinus' successor, for want of men, was forced to buy off the nearer threat, the Maeatae, who live just beyond the Forth, and so stop them from joining forces with the nations of the Caledonian heartlands beyond. However, within a few summers the same troublemakers were at it again, and this time only an imperial expedition could sort it out.

In those days, such an expedition was truly imperial. Indeed, I cannot find any reference to a greater land-force than that which assembled to invade Caledonia, or Pictland, as they now call it. In addition to the bulk of Britannia's mobile reserve, the emperor took with him his personal Guard, legionary detachments, and auxiliary regiments from several other provinces. It would appear that they penetrated, although with serious losses, almost as far as any Roman army has ever gone; in the early phases they followed the existing road-system, but beyond the Tay the metalled roads give out, and they had to rely on their scouts and the field-notes of previous commanders. Twice they made the long haul from friendly districts, through the Maeatian lands, into the depths of Caledonia; at first they met with success, the two halves of their army operating independently, but later, in the teeth of renewed opposition, they combined into one crushingly massive force. The rigours of the march did for Severus; when death claimed him here in York he was preparing for one last push, confident that outright victory was in his grasp. Unfortunately his unworthy son Caracalla abandoned all his conquests, including the innovative scheme of isolated coastal bases south of the Tay and the Forth, supplied by sea and more than 100 miles from the frontier wall.

Were it not for his son, who knows how long Severus' plans for frontier control might have lasted? Nothing that came before it quite matched it for originality; nothing that followed has attracted more than a line or two in the pages of history. At any rate, despite such swift abandonment, the Severan campaigns ushered in a period of tranquillity, unbroken even when Britain became part of the breakaway Gallic Empire [AD 260-273]. It ended only when a bid for independence

[AD 287-96] under the ex-admiral Carausius, and later his finance minister Allectus, brought down another imperial expedition, led by Constantius Chlorus, on our heads. Chlorus and his son, the future emperor Constantine, returned a decade later [AD 306] to deal with trouble in the north; unfortunately, Chlorus too died in York.

Around this time official reports begin to refer to the northern hostiles as *Picti* (although you and I know that they went under various names). At any rate, up to the time of Count Theodosius' campaigns, they figure in three or four brief situation-reports, mostly in association with the *Scotti*, and once [AD 360], they are laughably described as 'breaking the agreements on the frontier' – as if a Pict would ever admit to an agreement on any topic! But,

joking apart, it is clear there have always had to be 'arrangements' on the frontier, beyond the purely military requirements. Our spies beyond the frontier, whose treachery [in AD 367] precipitated the disaster that we ourselves had to address under the elder Theodosius, were part of a surveillance system that was put in place long before our days: we've always had to depend on cloak-and-dagger men operating behind the Wall, but we shall need more than spies to secure the hearts and minds of the frontier people in the months immediately ahead. How tragic that we cut back on cross-border contact after the last debacle!

So much for history. What, you may ask, about the maps and plans? Well, there's nothing, at any scale, later than the revised map of the Diocese made by governor Alypius

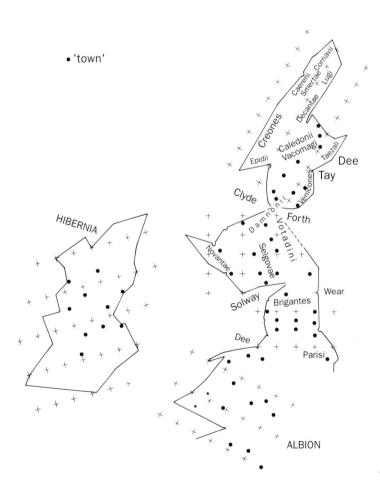

First-century Britain
Coastal and tribal information gathered during the Flavian advance and later compiled by Ptolemy of Alexandria, as it might have appeared in separate sheets, correctly aligned and with ten 'towns' per sheet.

[AD 357–360], and the only available road-book goes back 60 years before that to Diocletian! Looking at those old maps (neither of which shows much north of the Frontier Wall), it was strange to see a Britain that consisted of just three provinces, instead of the present five. Of course, for a hundred years before that, there were only two provinces, Inferior and Superior, and, amazingly, for the first 150 years of its existence, Britannia was under a unitary provincial control. Funnily enough, it was a map from that early period, which showed most clearly the home territories of those northern tribes with whom we are most concerned at present. The map comes in two versions: one that was published by the geographer Ptolemy in book format at Alexandria; and a second, presented in rather sketchy outline, illustrating the whole island (and Hivernia) on seven separate sheets, each indicating the ten most notable 'towns' (forts, I suppose) in the relevant district. Ptolemy's version has clearly been compiled from the other, but unfortunately some of the sheets have been joined to each other at the wrong angle, which gives an occasionally bizarre effect, especially as the scale also varies disconcertingly.

It is from the three northernmost sheets of this map that we learn the original names of our closest neighbours, the Novantae, Selgovae, and Votadini (who extend from west to east across the outer zone beyond our present frontier), as well as their neighbours, the Damnonii and Venicones, and the peoples of the Caledonian confederacy beyond. But, in my opinion, the most startling feature of these sheets is that they indicate as dense a deployment of Roman forts to the north of the Tyne-Solway isthmus as they do to the south. Since the latter area on the map

seriously under-represents the number of forts that were actually built, we must presume that a comparably dense pattern once extended right into Caledonia! I'm therefore convinced that there is a direct correlation between this intense northern activity and the bulging portfolios here in York, which contain blueprints for elaborate military installations of a size and type we never see these days. So it must be the camp-sites and stations of those early campaigners (and their immediate successors) whose eroded earthworks we can still trace beside the upland roads of the north country. These installations should now inspire us as we prepare for the coming redeployment. They were designed and built by armies in rigorous pursuit of well-defined objectives, and their classic form doubtless reflects this. And that, in turn, reflects the enormous respect the commanders of that time entertained for their northern adversaries. Since we too must shortly consider how best to handle matters with their descendants, may I recommend that you read carefully the accompanying memoranda on the works of the Eagles of old?

Farewell till we meet!

Forced Entry: Invasion and Conquest

'No one now for a long time has built a camp with a ditched perimeter and a stockade fixed above it'.
Flavius Vegetius Renatus, *Epitome of Military Science*, I, 21.

'The erection of the outer defence and the buildings inside it is accomplished faster than thought, thanks to the numbers and skill of the workers'.
Flavius Josephus, *The Jewish War*, Excursus III.

The evidence of the marching-camps

It is ironic that the invasions of Scotland by the Romans, whose immediate objective was to conquer and lay waste, should have left behind such a rich legacy. No other country can boast so wide a range or so many examples of structures built by the legions during their campaigns, when professional armies, often tens of thousands strong, advanced across the northern landscape. They went wherever duty or glory called; they stopped only when the day's march, or military quest, was ended. At the end of each day, they pitched their carefully-aligned rows of leather tents, each row in its set space and location within the defences

Roman Legions on the March
It is Spring, and the the army is on the move. As the rear of the column approaches the end of its day's march, legionaries of Agicola's army are hard at work completing the overlapping *claviculae* that protect the gate of the Stracathro-type marching-camp which will be their temporary base.
CHRIS BROWN

The View from Above

Aerial photographs of a Roman temporary camp (top) and a permanent fort (bottom), both in Dumfries and Galloway, are revealed by cropmarks. Over the buried ditches of the camp at Ward Law, the greener growth of corn defines the single-ditch perimeter; within the more complex defences of Glenlochar fort lighter tones indicate the internal street grid.
RCAHMS

of the camp: on occasion, a low bank of sods would have sufficed to defend it, but more often the camp was surrounded by a V-sectioned ditch, its size proportionate to the scale of danger faced, and within there stood a rampart crowned by the wooden stakes each soldier carried. It is little short of a miracle that any traces now survive of these temporary structures, so swiftly erected by the teams of diggers and spoil-shifters, that onlookers almost doubted what they saw. The rare quality and quantity of the Scottish material, in great part the result of decades of aerial survey, especially through the recording of cropmark evidence, allow archaeologists today not only to reconstruct the successive invasion routes, but also to figure out the intentions of those in command, and tentatively reconstruct the Order of Battle of the army.

But how can these sites yield such complicated information? At the lowest level, although most Roman camps share certain characteristics, resembling a playing-card on plan, with straight sides and rounded corners, there are various structural details – for example, the camp's proportions, the design or spacing of its gates, and possibly its relationship to other structures – which may indicate its date. When camps of the same size and appearance are found at regular intervals along a line of movement, we can assume they are marching-camps built by legionaries of the same battle-group as it advanced through enemy territory. Occasionally, however, we can deduce more, for in every instance the camp's appearance is determined by unseen operational requirements. Most obviously, its size is directly

related to the number and status of the troops it needed to accommodate: according to the military manual, each *contubernium*, or messing-unit, of eight legionaries, occupied a tent measuring 10 by 10 Roman feet (a Roman foot is about 296mm, compared with a British Imperial foot of 305mm). The six rows of 10 tents apiece required for a complete legionary cohort were assigned a tentage area measuring 120 by 180 Roman feet. Unfortunately, it is not clear how much space within any camp might have been allocated to such additional elements as equipment, draught animals, or indeed accompanying auxiliary troops (whose numbers usually matched those of the legionaries); nor is it known how much space was so 'awkward' as to be unusable.

Nevertheless, much can be gleaned from close scrutiny of the remains. The distance between each camp in a chain and the scale of the defences at each site should indicate the degree of danger faced by the invasion force; the identification of rows of rubbish-pits (flanking the lines of tents) will suggest a longer than overnight occupation and may furnish invaluable information about the camp's internal layout. Being the weak spots in the perimeter, since they lacked proper gates, the entrances frequently display structural features designed to lessen their vulnerability; the various flanking or covering devices employed for that purpose constitute further evidence of the perceived level of threat, but more importantly they gave scope to the individual legionary construction-teams scope to 'sign' their handiwork. Thus the wide range of marching-camps discovered in Scotland do more than just identify the strategic targets of ancient invasion forces or the areas of greatest resistance; their structure also reveals the nature of the forces that brought them into being, and the late first-century, or Flavian, examples are the most informative.

The Flavian campaigns (c. AD 77–83)

We are extremely lucky that the Roman campaigns in Scotland took place during the heyday of military field-engineering in Britain, long before the decline which Vegetius decried in the later fourth century (quoted at the beginning of the chapter); and we are luckier still that, when the governor Julius Agricola

Campaigning Before Agricola
The 8.1ha camp at Rey Cross, County Durham, on the line of march from York to Carlisle, belongs to a many-gated class of marching-camp possibly dating to the advance of Petillius Cerealis in AD 71-74. RCHME

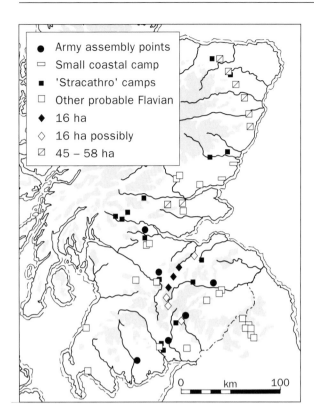

Legend:
- ● Army assembly points
- ⬭ Small coastal camp
- ■ 'Stracathro' camps
- ☐ Other probable Flavian
- ◆ 16 ha
- ◇ 16 ha possibly
- ▨ 45 – 58 ha

0   km   100

Where the Flavian Armies Marched
Map showing the distribution of
marching-camps that probably housed
the battle-groups engaged in North
Britain under the emperors Vespasian,
Titus and Domitian.

turned his attention c. AD 78/79 to the
annexation of the lands beyond Tyne and
Solway, he commanded an army which had,
over the previous decade or so, begun to
accustom itself to the discipline of regular
marching-camp construction. It is possible
that, in the first stages of their advance beyond
the Solway, Agricola's troops passed or even
re-used the camps built during the earlier
conquest of the lands of the Brigantes by
the governor Petillius Cerealis.

Several criteria can be used to identify
those marching-camps most probably the
work of Agricolan forces; they include a
tendency to squareness of plan, and a method
of gateway defence incorporating the *clavicula*
(an extended arc of ditch and rampart that
compelled an attacker to expose his
unprotected side to the camp's defenders).
Using these and other criteria we can show
that in southern Scotland Agricolan, or at
least Flavian, armies operated in strength in
most of the main river valleys, apparently
moving north from bases at Carlisle and near Corbridge on the
Tyne; the coastal districts of Lothian and Berwickshire seem to
have received scant attention, probably because the local people,
the Votadini, had adopted a pro-Roman policy, whereas the
reverse is true of the shores of Clyde and Solway. The largest
camps in eastern Scotland were some 16-20 hectares (ha) in
area, while those on the west occasionally attained 25ha.
(A hectare – roughly 2½ acres – equals 10,000 square metres, or
about two football pitches.) The actual distribution of camps is
uneven. Some clearly represent major lines of advance, for
example, the two claws of the pincer movement from mid-
Clydesdale and Northumberland towards the Forth. Others
appear in clusters, often beside river crossings, as at Newstead,
Castledykes, Beattock, and Dalswinton, identifying them as the
assembly points for armies engaged in the two years of
consolidation which followed.

One such cluster, on the south bank of the River Carron
near Camelon, marks the springboard for Agricola's ultimate
conquest of Caledonia, which Tacitus tells us was the objective
of his last two campaigns, in AD 82-83. The earliest penetration
of Caledonia, however, had been effected three years earlier in
Agricola's third campaign, when, we are told, the legions
advanced as far north as the Tay estuary. The cropmark traces of

two or three exceptionally large camps recorded in the lower valley of the Earn indicate the probable course of that push. Elsewhere north of the Forth, there is only one other instance of temporary camps revealing an Agricolan line of march – the series of seven camps that extends north and north-west in a great arc from near Stonehaven to the Pass of Grange, just east of the Spey, which I will discuss later. The dozen or so others are of widely differing size, doubtless representing a range of temporary duties which individual detachments might be called on to perform: fort-building (several adjoin *castella* of Agricolan date) and overseeing coastal installations, to name but two. Several are of a size and character, however, that point to a more significant role, especially given their location astride important natural corridors.

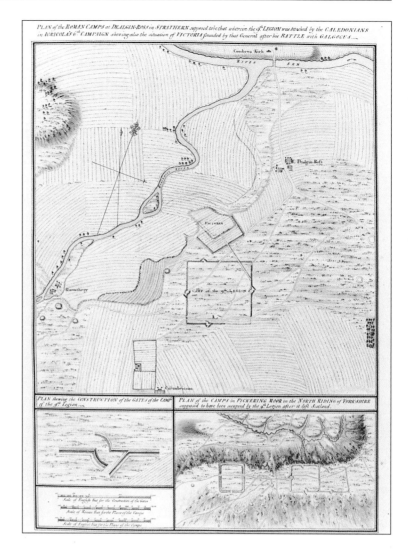

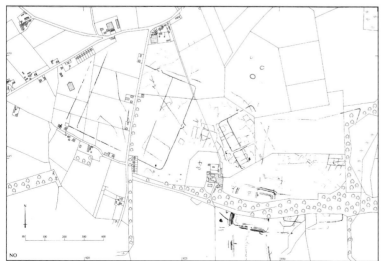

(above)
Early Plan of a Roman Site
Manuscript copy of the survey of the Agricolan fort and Stracathro-gated camp at Dalginross, near Comrie, made by William Roy in 1755. The inset (bottom left) shows the combination of *claviculae* and traverse.
SOCIETY OF ANTIQUARIES, LONDON

(left)
Gathering-ground for Eagles
Transcribed aerial photograph of the multiperiod Roman fort at Castledykes, near Carstairs in mid Clydesdale, with marching-camps of the various field-armies which halted here.
RCAHMS

All of the latter are further distinguished by a singular type of gateway defence, called the 'Stracathro gate' after the site south of Edzell in Angus where it was first recognised in cropmark form; its original appearance is nevertheless best illustrated by the examples at the camp of Dalginross, near Comrie in Perthshire, which was surveyed by General Roy in 1755, before the earthworks were levelled by cultivation.

The Stracathro entrance, featuring opposed *claviculae* and an oblique traverse, is found only in Scotland. Furthermore, its distribution in Scotland, though widespread, is localised in distinct areas – south-west Scotland, Strathclyde, central Scotland, Strathmore, and Aberdeenshire – corresponding to five of Agricola's six 'Scottish' campaign-areas, which suggests that it was the product of one particular legion engaged in those campaigns. There are good reasons to believe that the legion responsible was the Second Adiutrix, then based at Chester. It seems likely that both it and the Twentieth *Valeria Victrix*, from Wroxeter, were present at almost full strength throughout the Agricolan conquest of the north, together with a weakened Ninth *Hispana* (from York).

It was with these forces that Agricola approached the climax of his six-year governorship. We read in Tacitus that, after a campaign in which the cunning of the Caledonian warlords had almost engineered the slaughter of the unlucky Ninth Legion, both sides had determined that matters must be brought to a head. The North Britons had united under the leadership of an outstanding warrior named Calgacus, 'Swordsman', and taken up a position, allegedly more than 30,000 strong, on a hill which the Romans were to remember as *Mons Graupius*. Precisely where that field of battle lies cannot yet be determined. Nevertheless, if the chain of large marching-camps that curves through Aberdeenshire towards the Spey can be dated to the Flavian period, as their appearance suggests, it would be difficult to find a more appropriate context for them than the *Mons Graupius* campaign. Indeed, it has been proposed that the largest of the series (c. 57ha), situated at Logie Durno, facing the peak of Bennachie, directly adjoins the field of battle.

Regardless of the accuracy of that identification – and there are reasons for suggesting that the battle was fought even further to the north-west – the importance of Logie Durno lies in the information it may reveal on marching-camp capacity: basically, how many troops to the hectare. The Durno camp is significant because it is 13 to 14ha larger than the other camps in the series – a figure which appears quite frequently in temporary camp statistics. In this case it is the average area of the two camps with Stracathro gates (at Ythan Wells and Auchinhove) which housed a

The March to *Mons Graupius*?

The chain of marching-camps probably built by the two units of Agricola's army on their way north to the battle of *Mons Graupius* in AD 83. When united, as at Durno, opposite Bennachie, the army was possibly 40,000 strong.

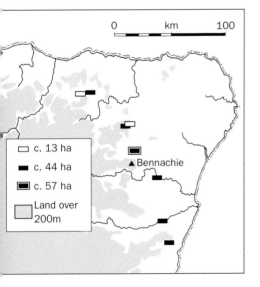

unit apparently accompanying the main force on this campaign, but, except at Durno, operating independently of it. At the site of Ythan Wells, one day's march to the north, the smaller 13-14ha camp was built over by the larger, indicating that there the minor detachment, representing about a quarter of the whole army, had led the advance. It is not unreasonable to presume that the smaller force was one that could easily have been split from the rest, in other words, a standard detachment based on a single legion (which the Stracathro gateways reveal as the Second *Adiutrix*). At neither Ythan Wells nor Auchinhove can an estimate readily be made

Legionary Labour-camp
Cropmarks reveal a uniquely detailed picture of the internal arrangements of the camp housing the builders of Inchtuthil fortress, to the south-west of Blairgowrie, Perthshire; the rows of dark dots indicate the rubbish-pits adjoining the legionary tent-lines.
RCAHMS

of the total troop strength involved, but comparison with another possible Second Legion product, the 9.4ha camp at Dalginross, is instructive. A combination of aerial photographic data with Roy's 1755 survey makes it possible not only to obtain a precise measurement of the camp's defences and internal structures, but also to deduce it was built to accom-modate the equivalent of a legion with little or no auxiliary support; the probability that Dalginross was not a marching-camp but a temporary base for local reconnaissance and intelligence duties makes such an assessment even more reasonable.

On this analysis, Ythan Wells and Auchinhove, with half as much capacity again as Dalginross, probably accommodated not only the full legion but also 2-3000 auxiliaries, or some 8000 men in total. In consequence, Durno would have held a combined force well in excess of 32,000, suggesting in fact that Agricola used all his resources to ensure victory over the Caledonians. The 13-14ha camps may therefore represent a not uncommon Agricolan troop-deployment, recorded by his son-in-law Tacitus as 'a legion and a modest force of auxiliaries'.

Similar links between tactical capacity and size or shape should doubtless be sought in other Agricolan camps. Thus, Stracathro itself, at 15.7ha, could have accommodated an auxiliary supplement equal in size to the legion it accompanied, or up to 11,000 in total, while Dalswinton or Castledykes, at 25ha, could

Dalginross from the Air
About 240 years of cultivation have removed the earthwork defences recorded by Roy (see page 19), but internal details of both fort and camp can now be revealed by cropmarks.
R.CAHMS

have accommodated more than 20,000 men, or two full legions each with a moderately large support force. Since it seems likely that the Ninth Legion would have contributed to the Agricolan advance by moving north from York, the two legions operating together to operate in the west of Scotland must have been the Second *Adiutrix* and the Twentieth (which contemporary records suggest may have left detachments at Carlisle). Until the final campaign, the respective legionary objectives are less easy to distinguish, although it is reasonably certain that the Second remained in the thick of things. It was not, however, the unit detailed to remain in Scotland as the garrison of the new fortress at Inchtuthil, on the banks of the Tay in Perthshire.

The two-phase construction-camp that housed the builders, and eventual occupants, of the new legionary fortress at Inchtuthil is probably the latest temporary enclosure of the Flavian period north of the Forth, dating perhaps to AD 84. In its earliest form, carefully positioned to avoid obstructing the direct route from the front gate of the fortress, the camp covered almost 20ha, an area sufficient, given the more relaxed peacetime conditions, for not only most of the legion that would eventually occupy the fortress, but also a generous support team. It is usually assumed that the future garrison was the Twentieth Legion, based until then at Wroxeter, a position which had become too remote from the action. Whatever the identity of the builders, aerial photography has recorded within the camp the cropmark traces of numerous rows of tent-line rubbish pits, confirming the lengthy period the building party spent under 'canvas', while they constructed the permanent defences and internal structures of the legionary base. Ironically, the 'permanent' fortress they laboured to build may have enjoyed an even shorter period of use than their temporary quarters; within a couple of years or so, due to events on the Danube frontier, one of Britain's four legions had to be sent abroad, and soon the fabric of the Agricolan victory began to unravel. Inchtuthil and all the northern conquests were abandoned, while Newstead on the Tweed, along with other forts in the south of Scotland, was refurbished to serve as forward positions on a new frontier.

The Antonine campaigns (c. AD 140–142)

'As far as possible, a camp's length should be half as much again as its width, to ensure that the lines have sufficient ventilation.' Hyginus, *On Building Camps*, 21.

The evidence relating to the campaigns that preceded the building of the Antonine Wall is totally different – not least in the apparent absence of serious activity north of the Forth. Gone is the variety of structures; in their place, we find only workmanlike regularity and uniformity, effective but unexciting. The Antonine camps are mainly distinguished by the more elongated plan of Hyginus, especially one in which the long side is half as long again as the short, and an avoidance of the *clavicula*; gateways were protected by a device also used in Agricolan camps, the *tutulus*, a detached bar of ditch and rampart set forward from the entrance to prevent direct assault.

The builders of the Antonine marching-camps evidently followed the pre-existing road in their operations, and frequently appear to have used the road embankment as the baseline from which to set out the camp fortifications. As a result their commanders were able to capitalise on experience gained during the Flavian advance. Knowing what to expect in the way of route-mileage and possible resistance, they could operate at the minimum necessary strength and calculate supply requirements to a nicety. The apparent inactivity of the tribes north of the Forth-Clyde isthmus meant that they did not need to maintain a large strategic reserve – their main objective was to secure what would become the hinterland of the new frontier, showing the Eagle in all the main centres of population, with field-forces usually well below their maximum disposable strength. The forces used were nevertheless large enough to indicate that a question-mark still hung over the loyalties of the peoples in southern Scotland and northern England. If camp area was still allocated in accordance with Flavian standards, the invasion force of AD 139-140 included units resembling Agricola's single legion with moderate auxiliary support (in c. 13ha camps), but more often it employed the individual legion with full support (in c. 16ha camps). On occasion, and particularly evident in the series of c. 20ha camps that adjoin Dere Street from between the modern Border and the Forth, larger groupings, possibly of more than one legion, were deemed necessary.

Three legions were available for duties in these operations: the Second *Augusta*, the Twentieth (now based at Chester), and the Sixth at York (replacing the departed Ninth). However, the characteristic regularity and uniformity of plan of the Antonine

Antonine Marching-camp
Typical of the camps of the second century, with its regular, elongated plan and six, tutulus-guarded gateways, Pennymuir, in the south-eastern Borders, aligns itself with the Roman road Dere Street, now a modern track visible to the left of the camp, along which its builders had advanced over the Cheviots.
RCAHMS

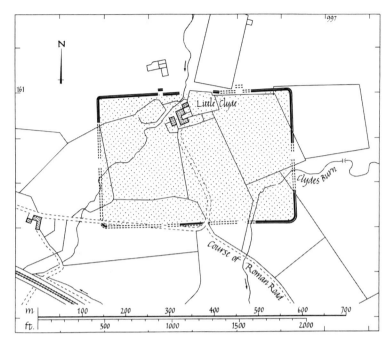

Regularity Before Everything
Little Clyde, situated on the watershed between Clyde and Annan, not only measures exactly 1000 by 1500 Roman feet over the rampart but also maintains a perfect rectangular plan, despite including within its perimeter the rocky gullies of two streams.
RCAHMS

Severan Marching-camps.
Ardoch (53ha) and Kirkbuddo (25ha) represent the two classes of early third-century camp found north of the Forth. Contemporary structures south of the Forth were 13ha bigger than Ardoch (top); the average permanent fort was about the size of the Kirkbuddo annexe (bottom).
GORDON MAXWELL, MERCAT PRESS

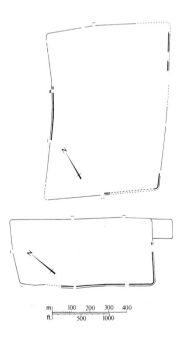

camps also make it difficult to distinguish between the products of different legionary drawing offices. The camp at Little Clyde, possibly one of the Second Legion's halts on the watershed between Clyde and Annan, splendidly illustrates the general appearance of the majority. It is a regular rectangle measuring precisely 1500 by 1000 Roman feet, its 13.2ha area being appropriate to a 'legion with moderate support'. Two features stand out: the greater number of gates, both long sides being provided with two; and the marked regularity of the plan, maintained despite the extremely broken nature of the ground occupied. The six entrances, a number found mostly only in the very largest Flavian camps, may reflect either the greater self-confidence of the Antonine legions or simply a desire to facilitate entry and exit.

The Severan campaigns (c. AD 208–212)

'The Britons having broken their agreements and taken up arms, Severus ordered his soldiers to invade their territory and put to the sword all that they met, adding the Homeric quotation that "they should let nobody escape, not even the children hidden in their mothers' wombs"'.
Cassius Dio, LXXVI, 16.

There is one significant difference between Antonine (second-century) and Severan (third-century) camps – their size. Whereas the Antonine examples rarely exceeded 20ha, we know of no Severan camps below 25ha; on the contrary, the two largest series average respectively 53ha and 65ha.

The Severan sites, in contrast to the Flavian, are all marching-camps associated with one of three campaigning phases. The four camps of the 65ha series indicate three successive days' march along Dere Street from the Tweed to the Lothian Tyne; each day, a journey of eight Roman miles was accomplished, a creditable distance for an army whose strength, based on camp-capacity already estimated, probably exceeded 40,000. Such vast numbers, comprising not only most of the British legions' strength together with auxiliaries, but also detachments of the Praetorian Guard and contributions from overseas legions, show that Severus' campaign was a truly majestic undertaking. Assuming some 25–30,000 of the army were on foot, and most of the cavalry were deployed off the road, Dere Street would have been packed with columns six files wide for up to three miles. The several hundred carts, carrying baggage and provisions for men and beasts, would have lengthened the column by another two miles. The advance party would have surveyed the next night's resting-place when the rear had barely caught its first wind on the march!

At some point beyond the northernmost c. 65ha camp at Pathhead in Midlothian, probably near the coastal base of Cramond, the Grand Army seems to have left a detachment to attend to matters on the Forth-Clyde line, and then regrouped for separate duties, for there are two separate categories of Severan camps in the country north of the Forth – c. 53ha and 25 ha. Significantly, the party left behind near Cramond accounted for a 13ha diminution of the available force – a reappearance of the 'legion with moderate support'. Of the two northern series, the 25ha camps are the earlier: however, their combined distribution pattern seems likely to represent two equal parts of the reduced army, operating separately.

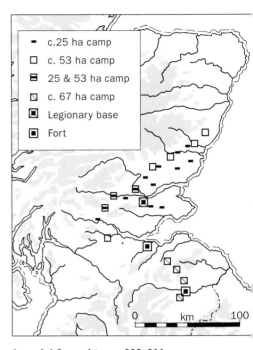

Imperial Campaigns AD 208–211
Temporary camp-sites indicate the route of Severus' army from the Tweed to the Forth and, in two equal units, throughout Caledonia. Over much of the area they are set a day's march apart.

- c.25 ha camp
- c. 53 ha camp
- 25 & 53 ha camp
- c. 67 ha camp
- Legionary base
- Fort

0   km   100

Trajan's Column
Trajan's column provides the most authoritative picture of the Roman army at the start of the second century – here it contrasts the second-line auxiliaries (left) and the elite soldiers of the legions (right).
ANGUS LAMB

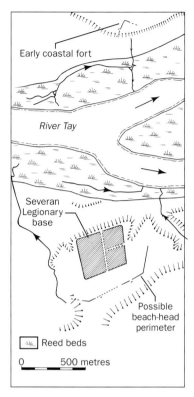

Third-century Coastal Stronghold

At Carpow on the south shore of the
Tay estuary aerial survey by the
University of Cambridge revealed not
only a Severan legionary base, but also
a polygonal ditched enclosure which
might possibly have defended the
beach-head of a Roman assault.
After St Joseph

Gold Coin

Aureus (gold coin) from the Severan
base at Carpow showing the head of
the Emperor Antoninus Pius, under
whom the Antonine Wall was built.
NATIONAL MUSEUMS OF SCOTLAND

The northernmost 25ha camps may thus belong to a
detachment pressing constantly north-eastward from the Teith
through Strathmore to the North Esk, and probably returning by
a coastal route.

The presumably simultaneous operations of the other half of
the army are less easy to interpret. It is possible to imagine a diver-
gence from the first group somewhere south of Ardoch, and then
an eastward march along the south side of the Earn to Carpow,
with subsequent forays into the heartland of Fife. However,
although an eastward advance is supported by the positions of the
camps at Auchtermuchty and Edenwood in Fife, Forteviot in
Perthshire, on the west bank of the Water of May, would appear
more likely to have been used by a force moving westward, that is,
returning to the Forth. The odd multi-sided enclosure at Carpow
has an important role to play here. Originally seen as a 25ha camp
somewhat deformed to cover the end of the bridge of boats used
to cross the Tay, but also explained as an outwork to the later
legionary fortress, its widely spaced gateways combine with the
available ground to suggest a capacity well in excess of 25ha.
Now, as there is roughly contemporary evidence pointing to the
involvement of elements from the fleets of three other provinces
in the British campaign, we may ask if Carpow should be
interpreted not as a bridgehead, but rather as a beachhead.

Since a legionary presence was eventually established here,
and almost certainly supplied by sea, why should the northern
campaigns not have included a seaborne assault? Intended to
divert attention from the land advance through Strathearn, and
directed at the rear of the Maeatae, the landings would have tied
up the potentially troublesome tribes of Fife, while the other part
of the army tackled the Caledonians. An operation on this scale,
involving the ferrying of almost 20,000 armed men, probably from
a temporary base on the Forth, would constitute one of the major
feats of the Roman army in Britain.

The operation was not repeated, for during the next campaign
the separate groups had to recombine in a renewed onslaught on
the now-rebelling Maeatae and Caledonians. The march of
this army, advancing relentlessly at an average of ten
miles a day along the inland route pioneered by
Agricola, has left, in the series of 53ha camps, one
of the most eloquent statements of Imperial power
to be seen anywhere in Britain. It is the track of
an army that methodically trampled everything
underfoot, even, as at Ardoch, the installations of
its predecessors, but certainly all foolhardy enough
to stand against the authority of Rome.

The Sinews of Power

'The effect of these operations was that many previously independent nations, who had laid down their arms and handed over hostages, were now guarded and watched over on all sides, with such judicious care, that they became part of the province of Britannia free from any external interference, something that had never happened before'.
Cornelius Tacitus, *The Life of Agricola*, 20, 3.

The aftermath of invasion

After each campaigning episode, especially during the Agricolan conquest, there was a period of consolidation during which assessments had to be made – of the population-density and the main natural resources of the conquered land, of the attitude of the different tribes to their conquerors, and of the vulnerability of the area to its unconquered neighbours. How best could the available Roman manpower be deployed to guarantee the security of the newly annexed territory, without prejudicing the prosperity and safety of the more settled areas?

What the situation called for, on the one hand, was a survey, to enable the effective 'farming' of the local economies, and thus defray the costs of maintaining an army of occupation; on the other, a thorough strategic review, to shake out the auxiliary garrisons, transferring them from relatively peaceful southern parts of the province. We must remember that this was a rolling process, with various stages. In AD 80–83, even while the advance moved north, fortified posts were being built for fixed garrisons, in some cases, not far behind the active war-zone. The size and nature of these *castella* and *praesidia,* as Tacitus calls them, have not yet been precisely determined.

Between Campaigns and Colonisation
Before regiments could be assigned to permanent bases, the garrison needs of newly overrun territory had to be assessed. The Flavian solution in southern Scotland apparently involved a provisional network of forts and intermediate fortlets.

The provisional network

Nevertheless, Agricola and his successor probably addressed this problem in a similar way, by sub-dividing units and spreading them out, to begin with perhaps more thinly than either might have wished. Newly conquered territory would have been overlaid by

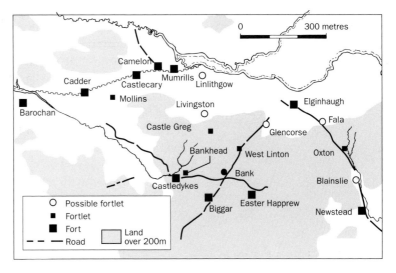

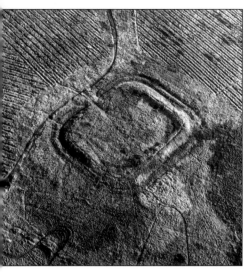

An Early Flavian Fortlet

On remote moorland, miles from any Roman road, forestry ploughing advances upon the earthworks of Castle Greg, Lothian, where the parrot's-beak ditch-terminals at its single entrance indicate an Agricolan origin.
RCAHMS

Off the Beaten Track

Faint cropmarks reveal the position of the square Flavian fortlet at Kirkland, a node in the provisional network, guarding a side-valley off Nithsdale, not far from Moniaive, Dumfries and Galloway.
RCAHMS

a provisional network of fortified posts in which smaller and larger garrisons alternated, so carving up the tribal lands into a pattern of fields, whose edges, as yet unprovided with regular roads, were patrolled by the locally stationed troops. Eventually, as the tide of war rolled further north, or as the perceived threat diminished, individual posts, or even lines of posts, might be abandoned, after perhaps only a matter of months. In such cases, we would expect the physical remains to be extremely slight, so making the site difficult to identify in modern times unless by aerial photography. The well-preserved early Agricolan fortlet of Castle Greg, which lies in isolated moorland on the north side of the Pentland Hills, miles from the Roman road network, represents a remarkable exception.

Further instances of abandoned early semi-permanent posts have been identified actually on the line of the later road-system: the sites at West Linton and Glencorse, Peeblesshire, on the route leading north-eastward from Biggar along the south side of the Pentland Hills, are particularly significant, being positioned at respectively one day's march and half a day's march from the Agricolan fort of Elginhaugh, Midlothian. Similar subdivision of standard fort-intervals can be identified on Dere Street between Elginhaugh and Newstead. The main characteristics shared by these posts appear to be the absence of elaborate defences or prolonged occupation, an area of less than 0.4ha, and a tendency to be spaced half a day's march (c. 10km) apart.

Communications by land

'Of course, the farther North you go the emptier are the roads. . . and the wind sings through your helmet-plume.'
Rudyard Kipling, *Puck of Pook's Hill*, 'On the Great Wall' 1906.

The next stage of occupation – the establishment of more permanent garrisons – meant that the communications requirements had to be addressed. The machinery of military government simply could not have functioned without adequate supplies of materials and information. These needs were met by a relatively sophisticated system of roads and watch- or signal-towers.

The roads and towers took longer to complete than the forts they linked, and in some areas (such as Strathmore in the Flavian period) the construction programme lagged two or three years behind that of the forts. However, the road network should be considered first, as probably the biggest capital expenditure project associated with the occupation. Until this strategic road system was built, the land routes used would have been tactical, following where possible in the tracks of the campaigning

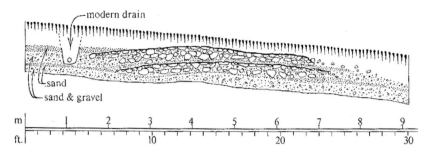

modern drain

sand

sand & gravel

columns and little altered from their natural state; pack-animals would have been used to transport materials, and only for important tasks would a specially engineered sector of road have been provided in advance of the main programme. During the construction of the legionary fortress at Inchtuthil, for example, a handsome wagon-road was laid to bring the stone from the distant quarries to the building-site. This road included a one-way loop, more than three Roman miles in extent, which ensured easier gradients for heavily laden wagons descending from the quarry, and restricted the more direct but steeper route to empty vehicles. If it took 6000 man-days to complete 10km of road of basic tactical standard (involving little more than clearing vegetation, filling in holes, and essential rock cutting), the scale of surveying, designing, and constructing more than 400 Roman miles (590km) required for the Agricolan conquest is almost unimaginable.

Given that much of the road-making took place in the frequently harsh environment of the Scottish uplands, the resulting product was remarkably uniform. Two-thirds of the system was apparently built to a standard carriageway-width of 20 Roman feet (5.9m), but what one might term the central spine of the road system, Dere Street, exhibits a more generous standard, perhaps as wide as 25-30 feet; the quarry-roads at Inchtuthil were of a similar standard.

A wide variety of construction techniques was used, reflecting the changing character of the terrain through which the roads ran. In areas with well-drained and firm subsoil little effort would be made to provide boulder bottoming – only enough to ensure the correct cambered profile. On softer ground, the road builders either excavated down to the bedrock, as on Craik Moor, or 'floated' the road mound on a raft of sand or gravel, as occasionally on the Biggar-Elginhaugh sector.

The Well-beaten Track
A cross-section of the Roman road to the east of Castledykes in Clydesdale, showing the two periods of smooth, cambered running-surface, with boulder bottoming, and underlayer of gravel bedding.

Straight as a Rule
A typical stretch of Roman road, with cambered running-surface flanked by rows of quarry-pits, is seen to advantage in this aerial view, as it crosses uncultivated upland on the south-east slopes of the Pentland Hills.
RCAHMS

(right)

The Earliest Quarry-road in Scotland

The Y-fork of the one-way road-system that linked the legionary base at Inchtuthil with the source of its building stone is indicated by cropmarks. The chains of darker splodges show where pits were dug to produce road material; the course of the road itself is revealed by an intermittent paler band.

RCAHMS

(below)

The Road Network

The securely identified sectors of the Roman road-system of all periods, together with coastal installations possibly associated with Flavian military operations.

□	Fort (probable)
■	Fort
■	Legionary Fortress
○	Possible Roman harbours
- - -	Roman Roads
▨	Land over 200m

Dun

Invergowrie

Carpow

Camelon

Dumbarton

Irvine

Girvan

Stranraer

0   km   100

Most of the material for bottoming and metalling came from roughly circular or oblong quarry-pits flanking the road and lying 5-15m from it. Typically 3-8m across and originally about 1.3 mdeep, the pits, in places, are so numerous that they overlap, suggesting that some may have been dug by later road-repair gangs. Where the roads have been heavily denuded by later activity, such pits may be the only evidence of the road's existence and its Roman origin: mere straightness of alignment is not evidence that a road is Roman – many eighteenth-century and later roads share this characteristic.

The road system fulfilled its function superbly: it ensured the safe, economical, and reasonably swift movement of men and material between the military establishments. The design of the road was governed by the needs of its most important traffic – wheeled vehicles. The worst gradients encountered on Roman roads in Scotland were about 1 in 4, but only infrequently and for short distances, while slopes of 1 in 6 seem the maximum generally allowed for longer climbs. Traffic negotiating such slopes would have been considerably aided by the generous road-width;

Take the High Road
In the valley of the Daer Water, upper Clydesdale, the dying rays of the midsummer sun pick out the quarry-pits, artificial shelf and cambered mound of the Roman road as it climbs towards the watershed, avoiding the deeply scooped house-platforms of an earlier age.
RCAHMS

as shown by the wheel-ruts in roads at Inchtuthil and other Roman sites, wagons were probably built to a standard gauge of 4ft 8 inches [British Imperial] (1.42m) and on the normal 20ft-wide Roman carriageway, it would have been quite possible to pass on-coming or slower-moving vehicles.

The road system would also have greatly eased the passage of information – the reports, returns, and requisitions upon which the Roman army, like the modern, depended for its very existence. As is shown by the correspondence recovered at Vindolanda on Hadrian's Wall, paperwork and the military mind are connected by an indissoluble link, and the official couriers responsible for its dispersal back and forth along the roads were further burdened by personal letters. For more immediate transmission of urgent or sensitive information, a totally different channel was required, an extensive system of intervisible towers. The means of transmission ranged from beacon-fires and trumpet-call to elaborate semaphore, and its speed of operation would have been invaluable in an emergency.

Heavy Goods Vehicles
The Roman road system was designed to accommodate wheeled traffic, including such ox-drawn wagons as appear on Trajan's column.
ANGUS LAMB

Telecommunication in Roman times

'And some hang wooden arms on the towers of forts and cities, to indicate what is going on by alternately raising and lowering them.'
Flavius Vegetius Renatus, *Epitome of Military Science*, III, 5.

All of the known examples of towers in Scotland were massively built timber structures, two or three storeys high, and most were roughly square in plan, with sides 10-12 Roman feet long; they were enclosed within one or two penannular ditches, and sometimes also protected by a rampart. Their close resemblance to the towers that flanked or surmounted the gateways of permanent forts may indicate, in some cases, that they were built by the same work party. Although a few are found in high positions, for example, on the summit of the North Eildon Hill, most adjoin a sector of the Roman road system. The towers had a twofold role: to see and be seen, that is, to serve both as watch-towers (particularly evident when they appear in a close-set series) and signal-towers. The best example of the former role, dating to the Flavian period, is known as the Gask frontier, after the ridge south-west of Perth along which it runs. Here, towers were integrated with forts and fortlets to maintain a close watch over an extended front which may originally have been drawn from the Forth to the banks of the Tay. News of hostile movements across or along this line (which may partly have coincided with a tribal boundary) would have been passed down the chain of posts with requests for immediate action.

The four examples in the sector of the Gask 'frontier' to the north and south of the fort at Ardoch merit particularly close attention. As a group, they are remarkable in their uniformity, being of similar size and spacing – 40 Roman

To See and Be Seen
Reconstruction drawing of a typical Flavian watch-tower.
HISTORIC SCOTLAND;
MICHAEL J MOORE

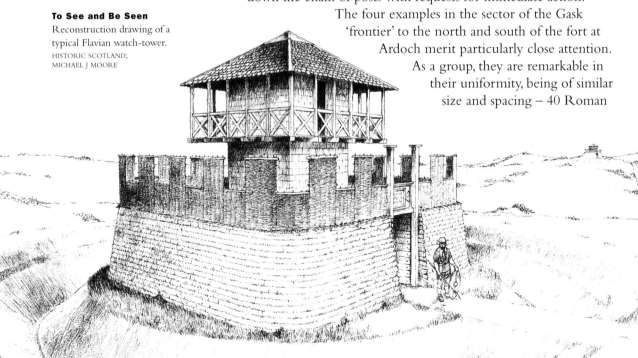

feet (over the rampart) and enclosed by double ditches; at the centre of each, occupying a quarter of the 20ft square interior, stood a 10ft square tower. It would be hard to imagine a more obviously modular product of a Roman military drawing office. Each tower was not only built by the builders of Flavian Ardoch, but also manned by the unit serving at Ardoch. The tower-detachment strength cannot be proved, but all the likely duties of the watch could have been adequately performed by a single *contubernium*, or messing-unit, of eight men; the tower's ground-space of 100 sq. ft, with at least one room above, would approximate to the barrack space allocated to this unit in the fort.

We know much less about the Antonine equivalents of such towers. Only two free-standing towers of that date have so far been identified – Beattock Summit and White Type. Built on a smaller scale than the Flavian towers, they lie, five Roman miles apart, on either side of the 2nd-century fortlet of Redshaw Burn, watching over the road that straddles the watershed between Clyde and Annan.

For more instructive parallels we must look to the Antonine Wall; yet even here only little understood fragments of the signalling system can be identified. The best-known groups comprise pairs of platforms abutting the south side of the Wall itself: one pair lies on each side of the fort at Rough Castle, and one to the west of the fort and fortlet on Croy Hill. The pairs are reckoned to have operated in combination, transmitting and receiving messages by beacon-fire to and from the Wall's eastern

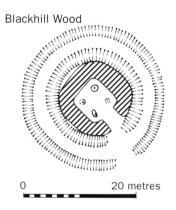

Blackhill Wood

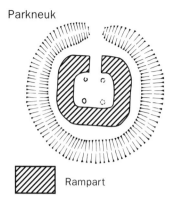

Parkneuk

0   20 metres

▨ Rampart

Peas in a Pod
Comparative ground-plans of two types of watch-tower on the Flavian frontier, as they might have been filed in the engineers' drawing-office of each respective legion.

Similar Function, Similar Form?
The communications needs of the second-century Walls were similar to those of earlier frontiers, the role of the watch-towers being discharged by turrets on Hadrian's Wall (right), and, on the Antonine Wall, by 'expansions' (middle) and possibly minor enclosures (left), all of comparable 'internal' area.

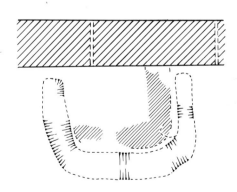

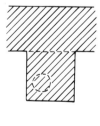

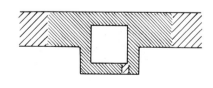

0   10 metres

Integrated Watch and Ward
The southern sector of the Forth-Tay frontier demonstrates how, in the Flavian period, surveillance and communication were maintained by complementary series of towers, fortlets, and various sizes of fort.

outposts and western hinterland. The nature of their super-structure, which was of turf, cannot be determined, but they were raised on stone-edged bases 18 Roman feet (5.2m) square. Resembling these in some respects, is the group of three minor enclosures discovered during aerial survey beside the Wall-fortlet of Wilderness Plantation; they too abut the south face of the Wall, but are defined by a single rampart and ditch, enclosing a space about 20 Roman feet square. From the excavation of one example little was learned, save that, like the Flavian towers of the Gask Ridge, or the stone turrets on Hadrian's Wall, a square module of 20 Roman feet appears significant in their construction; we may deduce that they had a related purpose.

Naval communications

'So one legion was detailed to each of the fleets at Misenum and Ravenna. . . with the capacity to go by sea, without delay or detour, anywhere in the world. . . for in wartime speed is usually more useful than courage.'
Flavius Vegetius Renatus, *Epitome of Military Science*, IV, 31 (Precepts of Naval Warfare).

Communication by water is often mentioned in accounts of Roman Scotland, but seldom substantiated by hard evidence. Yet the major role played by the *Classis Britannica* (the fleet of Britain) in Agricola's campaigns, whether in reconnaissance or tactical support, suggests that the advantages of water-borne transport would not have been ignored. We have little evidence other than an anchor allegedly found near Camelon, Falkirk, and

a possible steering-paddle discovered at Newstead. It is also true that, apart from the still-unconfirmed forts at Stranraer and Irvine (Rerigonium and Vindogara), few Agricolan installations are situated within walking distance of the seacoast, far less exploit natural harbours there. Indeed, reviewing the known Lothian sites, where Dere Street approaches the Forth, it is significant that a specifically inland route appears to have been chosen in the Flavian period; coastal positions like Inveresk and Cramond lay undeveloped until the second century.

On the other hand, with such major navigable rivers as the Forth or Tay penetrating deeply into the interior and offering the possibility of transhipment of cargoes to shallower-draught vessels, the army may not have got round to harbour construction before the withdrawal of AD 86/87. However, the reference in Ptolemy to a base called *Horrea Classis* implies that, somewhere on the coast of Fife, Perthshire, or Angus, a supply base was maintained for the Roman fleet in British waters, at least temporarily. Such a base would presumably have required a larger defensive perimeter than is found in such small camps as Dun on the Montrose Basin.

The only camp of reasonable size to occupy ground near enough the coast to justify a connection with naval operations is at Invergowrie, on the western outskirts of Dundee; however, the camp overlooks a coastline that has been much altered in recent centuries, and its capacity to provide safe harbourage in the past is largely unknown. The possibility that a Flavian naval base underlies the third-century works at Carpow a little way

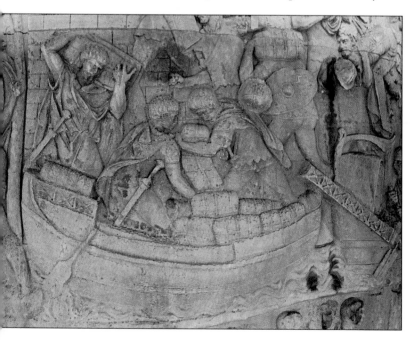

Waterborne Suppliers
Whenever practicable, Roman commanders would have used the fleet to supply forward positions as shown here on Trajan's column.
DAVID BREEZE

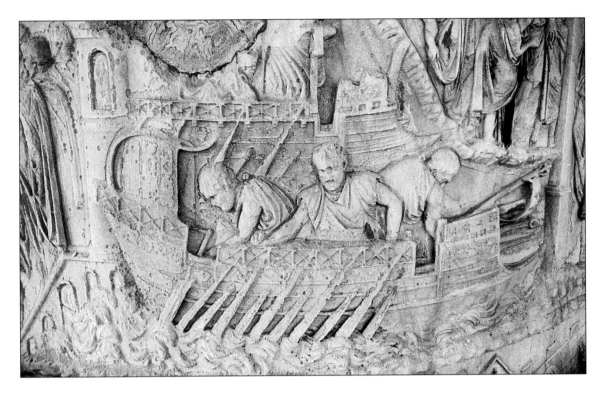

Roman Sea-power

In both communications and offensive operations, the Roman fleet in British waters *(Classis Britannica)* had as important a role to play as Danubian units in Trajan's war against the Dacians.
ANGUS LAMB

upstream on the opposite shore of the Tay, has often been considered, but since no early artefacts have come to light during excavations there, only a temporary landing-site seems feasible for the Agricolan campaigns. Perhaps it is just such an ephemeral installation that appears on Ptolemy's map; the very presence here in the Severan period of an isolated fortress, supplied by sea, demonstrates that such a location was a practical proposition.

No harbours have as yet been identified in the Flavian west, nor have any which may have accompanied the building of the Antonine Wall. There are, however, traces of a chain of second-century fortlets which follows the heights above the southern shore of the Clyde estuary and, reaching the sea near Largs, could have linked up with whatever military dispositions Agricola had earlier made from Irvine south to Stranraer. The discovery of such coastal installations might cast light upon one of Tacitus' more enigmatic observations – that Agricola was 'obsessed' with the possibility of an invasion of Ireland. The political pretext for this adventure – the arrival of a refugee Irish princeling – was no less fanciful than that which Claudius had exploited for the invasion of Britain in AD 43. There is thus a good chance that these unconfirmed western harbours were selected as the invasion bases for some never-realised naval assault.

Occupation

If communications-chains represented the sinews of the Roman occupation, the muscles were provided by the individual garrisons. And like the muscles of the human body, the garrisons of Roman Scotland differed in size and character depending on their function. As with the temporary camps, the Flavian permanent sites offer a key to understanding comparable installations of succeeding occupations. We have already looked at the physical remains of the Flavian watch-tower system that adjoins long stretches of the Forth-Tay road. Closer examination of the same sector will furnish us with illustrations of similar relationships, but on a larger scale.

Flavian fortlets

We noted earlier that a *contubernium* of eight men was probably adequate to operate each of the watch-towers in the vicinity of the fort at Ardoch. Fortlets were also an integral part of the system. The Ardoch-sector examples, Kaims Castle and Glenbank, both measure about 120 by 100 Roman feet (35m by 30m); the long axis of one lies at right angles to the road, that of the other parallel to it. On the analogy of the similarly sized, but later, fortlet at Barburgh Mill in Nithsdale, they would have accommodated a century of infantry, ten times the presumed strength of the tower garrisons. A clue to the relative capacities is provided by the spacing between neighbouring structures, which in this sector (unlike elsewhere on the Gask frontier) is a regular 3000 Roman feet, regardless of the type of structures at which the stage terminates. Since Kaims and Glenbank are very nearly six Roman miles (30,000ft) apart, it would seem that the ten intervals thus defined match the ten *contubernia* that make a century, and thus the theoretical density of deployment over each six-mile stretch was two centuries or 160 men: one in the fortlet, the other divided between the towers.

It was once thought that subdividing of garrisons and closer positioning of fortified sites was what distinguished a formal frontier from a standard communications route. However, recent study of fortlet types suggests strongly that these differences have a more complex origin, stemming sometimes from shortage of resources or purely temporary need. Mollins, to the south-west of Cumbernauld, at 60 metres square (0.4ha) is typical of the larger Flavian fortlets; probably one of Agricola's Forth-Clyde frontier chain of AD 80-81, it belongs to a group that seems equally at home in rural backwaters and on the front line.

Flavian Forth-Clyde Frontier

Air photograph of the large fortlet at Mollins, one of a chain of posts drawn by governor Julius Agricola across the Forth-Clyde isthmus during his fourth campaign.

RCAHMS

Flavian forts

Subdivision of standard military units need not be expected solely among the smaller classes of installations. Excavation at Strageath, the next fort north of Ardoch, revealed that, during all periods of occupation, the garrison comprised one complete regiment of auxiliaries and part of at least one other. The early investigation of Ardoch itself indicated that the mixed garrison there might include a legionary detachment. The presence in Flavian times of fractions of whole units at both sites would be totally understandable if they represented the residue left after detailing men to serve in the adjacent towers and fortlets. We have long known from actual unit reports such as those found at Vindolanda on Hadrian's Wall, that regiments were quite frequently well below their supposed strength. Since excavation at Strageath not only confirmed this but even suggested that the internal buildings of forts might have been designed from the beginning to accommodate only such reduced units, it might appear nearly impossible to use fort size alone to assess garrison strength, especially as different kinds of garrison – infantry, cavalry, and composite regiments – had different accommodation needs. However, the adoption of a rule-of-thumb approach by construction parties in the field seems to have had the perhaps unexpected effect of standardising fort size. The small Agricolan fort at Crawford (0.8ha), for example, which may have held half a cohort of mounted infantry, is the physical equivalent of two fortlets of the Mollins type set side by side. Although incapable of holding a complete regiment, excavation revealed that Crawford possessed a standard headquarters-building; it is therefore convenient to class it as a fort rather than a fortlet, despite its restricted capacity.

Bases for Sub-units

Computer-generated ground-plans from air photographs of Flavian installations near Ardoch – two types of watch-tower (1 and 2), and the small fortlets at Glenbank (3) and Kaims Castle (4), compared with the large fortlet at Inverquharity (5), by Kirriemuir, Angus.

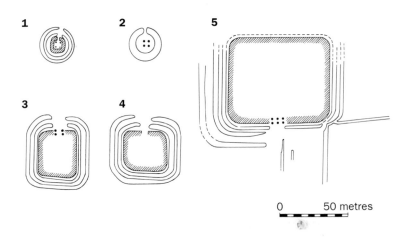

Elginhaugh, guarding the point where Dere Street crosses the North Esk west of Dalkeith, demonstrates the advantages and disadvantages of using fort-size to estimate garrison-size. Measuring about 445 by 405 Roman feet (132m by 120m) over the rampart (1.6ha), it represents, both in physical appearance and capacity, the equivalent of two forts of the type found at

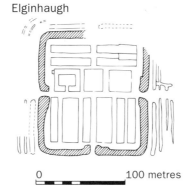

Elginhaugh

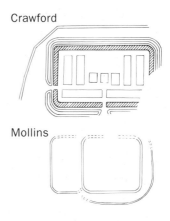

Crawford

Mollins

0   100 metres

Crawford built side by side; and yet excavation has shown that the interior, packed with timber buildings, accommodated many more troops than size, or comparison with Crawford, would have led us to believe. However, there are hints in the layout of the buildings that a less densely packed interior was originally planned.

Roman forts, like temporary camps, can also be classed according to their stylistic features. Inturned gateways, intended to make attacks on the entrance more difficult, are relatively common in early Roman fort architecture. This depth of defence could be achieved by recessing the flanking gate-towers some way back from the line of the rampart, often creating a long corridor of approach, or else by incurving the rampart itself. An alternative method was to provide a double or triple ditch system outside the rampart. By uniting and incurving the ditches on either side of the entrance, a funnelled approach was created in the form of an opposed pair of what are called 'parrot's beaks'.

Graded Garrison-posts

Evidence of a modular approach to fort construction in Flavian times provided by the large fortlet of Mollins, the small fort of Crawford, and the fort at Elginhaugh, each increase doubling the area available for use.

Discovery and Excavation

The initial aerial view (left) of the fort at Elginhaugh, where Dere Street crosses the North Esk, near Dalkeith, reveals only the parchmarks of the external and internal roads. When completely excavated (right), post-trenches for timber buildings appear everywhere within the interior.
RCAHMS

The 'parrot's beak' type of gate has advantages for the archaeologist: it can be recognised easily in cropmark form and it can be reasonably accurately dated, for at no site is it associated with structures later than the Flavian period. Its geographical distribution within Britain, on the other hand, is relatively wide, aerial survey having greatly increased the number of sites recognised. There are quite distinct groupings in Scotland, with particular frequency in the south-west, central Scotland, and in Strathmore; they are totally absent from the south-east. Since this distribution pattern agrees broadly with that of the Stracathro-gated type of camp, the 'beak' may also indicate the handiwork of the Second *Adiutrix* Legion. This suggests that legionary command responsibilities endured from the campaigning stages through to at least the initial phase of the occupation. To confirm this association we must look to the seven or eight known or suspected sites in England and Wales; their restricted distribution in north Lincolnshire/south Yorkshire, as well as in north Wales/Lancashire points unequivocally to the activities of the Second Legion, transferred from the lower Rhine to Lincoln around AD 71 and moved across to Chester some time before Agricola's governorship.

The 'parrot's beak' gates in several of the forts in Strathmore – at Cardean, Cargill, and possibly at Stracathro, shows that the Second Legion was active in the north up to and perhaps beyond the end of Agricola's Caledonian campaigns. As to its status when the

Timber Gateway of Flavian 'Parrot's-beak' Fort

At many of the earthwork-and-timber forts which housed the auxiliary regiments of the Agricolan garrison in Scotland the gateways are accompanied by 'parrot's beak' ditch-terminals, possibly an indication that they were built by the legion also responsible for the construction of 'Stracathro' camps.

CHRIS BROWN

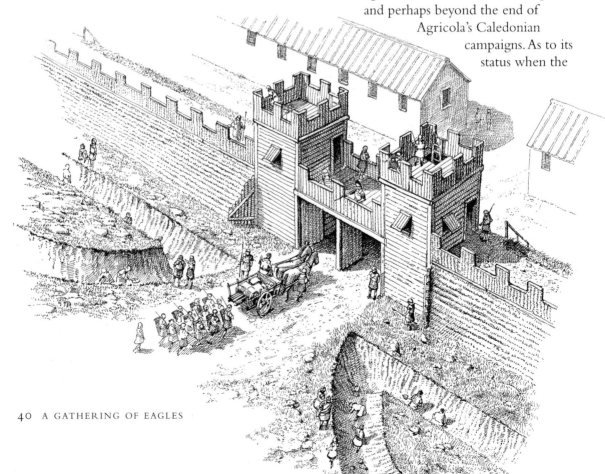

withdrawal from the northernmost conquests was ordered in AD 86/87, the evidence is ambiguous. The defences of the last period at Dalswinton, Bankhead, in Nithsdale, did not use the 'beak'; at Milton, Annandale, on the other hand, both the early and the later defence-systems employed the device. On balance, it seems likelier that, by this stage, the Second Legion was on its way to the Danube; shortly afterward, facing the inevitable, Rome had decided to abandon all the Agricolan conquest.

Antonine frontier policy

'Through the actions of his lieutenants, Antoninus waged a great many wars: on his behalf Lollius Urbicus, the provincial governor, conquered the Britons, having driven off the barbarians and built another wall, of turf.'
The Augustan History, Antoninus Pius, V.

When the legions marched north again almost 40 years later, new officers and new ideas had appeared in the field of military engineering, and the effect was noticeable. Authority decided that if a line now had to be drawn between Caesar's land and *barbaricum*, the new line had to be a physical barrier which could fittingly express the superiority of Rome, rather than a chain of discrete garrisons. The Antonine Wall was certainly 'physical': for over 40 Roman miles its turf-faced rampart snaked, 10ft high and 14ft thick, along the escarpments and crags marking the southern side of the Central Scottish Rift Valley, with a massive ditch in front and a Military Way behind. Abutting its southern side were at least 17 forts, about 40 fortlets, and an unknown number of lesser installations, while at intervals, embedded in each face, stood handsomely carved stone tablets, Distance Slabs that recorded the completion of successive sectors of Wall-building by individual legions.

Legionary Trademarks
At Malling, on the Lake of Menteith, the auxiliary fort with its conspicuous parrot's-beak gateway and (to the left) the Stracathro-gated marching-camp display the equivalent of architectural signatures, possibly those of the Second Adiutrix Legion.
RCAHMS

The Turf Curtain
On the Antonine Wall, running from Bo'ness in the east to Old Kilpatrick on the west, there were at first six forts and about forty fortlets. This plan shows it in its final, much strengthened form.

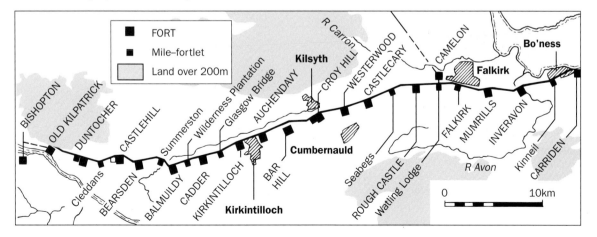

(above)

Arthur's O'on

At the end of another season in the field, early in the Antonine occupation, the senior staff officers of the Second Augustan Legion attend a *suovetaurilia* (sacrifice of pig, sheep, and bull) to celebrate the successful completion of the Wall-building task. The scene, depicted on the Bridgeness Distance Slab, has been transferred to the temple of Victory on the opposite side of the Forth at Stenhouse, whose imposing remains later generations called Arthur's O'on (Oven).

CHRIS BROWN

Vanished Glory

The Roman temple known as Arthur's O'on (Oven) on the banks of the Carron, which was barbarously demolished to provide material for the dam of an early ironworks, is here seen in a sketch made by the eighteenth-century antiquary and surveyor William Roy.

SOCIETY OF ANTIQUARIES, LONDON

The most magnificent of these slabs was set up by the Second *Augusta* Legion at Bridgeness, in Bo'ness, probably at the eastern end of the frontier. It bears two carved panels, one depicting a victorious cavalryman, the other a religious ceremony, which conveyed to a conquered population the same propaganda message as the Wall itself: that the combination of military might and divine favour made Rome irresistible. Although divine favour may lack relevance in modern times, to a Roman the sacrifice to Victory depicted on the Bridgeness slab would have demonstrated the renewal of a living contract between Rome and her gods at the end of a successful campaign. The same ceremony may well have been performed by officers of the Second Legion at Arthur's O'on, a possible victory monument or temple of Antonine date, which long survived at Stenhouse on the other side of the Forth, some nine miles to the west, only to be deliberately destroyed in 1743.

The Flavian armies would never have dreamt that a continuous curtain of walling would one day replace the open frontiers, yet there were elements of the new Antonine frontier which they would certainly have recognised. The most significant of these would have been the forts and intervening fortlets supplemented by occasional watch-towers. In its original form the frontier had six forts, set half a day's march apart, linked not only by the curtain wall with its sentry-walk, but also, at roughly one-mile intervals, by fortlets. At an early stage this system had

Imperial Propaganda
The easternmost Distance Slab on the Antonine Wall, at Bridgeness, is also the largest and most impressive. The dedication to the Emperor Antoninus Pius, recording the building of 4652 paces of the Wall by the Second Augustan Legion, is flanked by scenes of victory and ritual sacrifice.
NATIONAL MUSEUMS OF SCOTLAND

View of the Antonine Wall at Croy Hill
Winter is drawing on. In the lee of the Antonine Wall on Croy Hill and looking north-west we can see that the original fortlet has now been replaced by a fort; in the foreground, soldiers of the Sixth Legion, engaged in either repair work or support duties, gather in the garrison cemetery to attend the funeral of a comrade.
CHRIS BROWN

been strengthened by the addition of about a dozen forts, each about two miles apart. The density of garrisons might have appalled, and the wide range of plans and sizes bemused, a visitor from the past; he might also have looked in vain for evidence of a comprehensive series of watch-posts. But the fortlets he would have known and understood. Although smaller than most first-century examples and manned by garrisons not more than half a century strong, with their towered gateways the fortlets would not only have fulfilled the 'see and be seen' role that was the mainstay of the earliest defence-lines; they would also have served as architectural 'signatures' of the separate legionary parties at work on the Wall, since each Legion's fortlets were built on a slightly different plan. The Twentieth Legion apparently built fortlets whose short axis lay at right angles to the Wall-curtain, whereas in the fortlets of the Second Legion it was the long axis that was so aligned.

Of course, the association between legionary troops and the Wall did not end with the building phase; some played a role in its eventual manning, but not necessarily in the sectors they had built. Thus, at the long-axis fort at Croy Hill, possibly built by the Second Legion, a Sixth Legion presence is also attested by building dedications and, more grimly, a tombstone. Does this mean that a legionary engaged in building the fort which replaced the fortlet died during the construction-work? Or was it a centurion who had stayed behind to command the fort's auxiliary garrison?

Turning to the area to the south of the Wall, we shall find further parallels to the Flavian experience, which confirm that comparable stimuli tend to produce comparable responses. Antonine Crawford in upper Clydesdale, for example, differed

Roman Gravestone

A gravestone found at Croy Hill depicting three legionaries.

NATIONAL MUSEUMS OF SCOTLAND

Frontier Modifications

Plan of the Antonine Wall near the summit of Croy Hill, showing the primary fortlet on the west, and the slightly larger fort which soon replaced it, overlying the site of an enclosure that may have belonged to an even earlier phase of Antonine occupation.

GLASGOW ARCHAEOLOGICAL SOCIETY

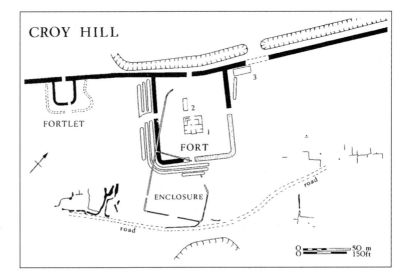

CROY HILL

FORTLET

FORT

ENCLOSURE

road

road

0
0 ━━ 50 m
150ft

minimally in size and shape from its Agricolan predecessor, and, although its interior layout was completely redesigned, it still contained a standard headquarters building and half-size barracks sufficient for half a 500-man auxiliary regiment. In this period it did not stand alone; dispersed around it in the upper valleys of the Clyde, Annan, and Nith, were earth-and-timber fortlets which would not have looked out of place on the turf section of Hadrian's Wall. In close association with one of these, the fortlet at Redshaw Burn, we have already seen that a pair of timber watch-towers maintained surveillance along the road; so slight are their remains, that many others, now destroyed, may once have lined the roads that linked the fortlet chain. How many of these recognised Crawford as their mother-fort we cannot tell. Doubtless some were manned by detachments from larger forts, like recently discovered Ladyward to the west of Lockerbie or Drumlanrig in upper Nithsdale. The existence of this integrated system unambiguously identifies this part of south-west Scotland as a potential threat to frontier security – not least because of its proximity to the once-troubled kingdom of Brigantia; the scale of that threat may possibly be better indicated by the remarkable site at Burnswark in eastern Dumfriesshire.

(above)
High Passes and Lonely Outposts
An aerial view of the well-preserved Antonine fortlet near Durisdeer, Dumfries and Galloway, protecting traffic on a remote sector of the road from Clydesdale to upper Nithsdale.
RCAHMS

(left)
A Monument for Posterity
In some stretches, as here at Watling Lodge, near Falkirk, where the ditch has survived centuries of erosion, we can understand why early post-Roman peoples thought the Antonine Wall was the work of a superhuman race.
HISTORIC SCOTLAND

Burnswark, a firing range for Roman field-artillery

'The artillery-pieces of all the legions were superbly constructed. . . their stone missiles weighing thirty kilos travelled 400m or more, and no one who got in their way remained standing. The enemy look-outs, posted on towers, gave warning whenever an artillery shot came hurtling towards them, with a shout of "Baby on the way!"'
Flavius Josephus, *The Jewish War*, V, 6.

Burnswark in lower Annandale constitutes a treasury of archaeological evidence, which illustrates aspects of Roman military activity seldom represented by upstanding field-monuments. Situated on the steeply sloping south face of Burnswark Hill, the complex commands a wide view southwards to the Solway and Cumbria. It comprises a Roman long-axis fortlet, a temporary camp, and various types of minor settlement of the local population, as well as a number of possible post-Roman burials; a smaller Roman camp, of irregular plan, is sited at the foot of the Hill's northern slope. The distinctively shaped summit of the Hill is occupied by an equally wide range of structures, dating from the early prehistoric to the mediaeval and later periods. Of these, the most relevant to this account is the hillfort whose timber-revetted ramparts once enclosed the entire summit area (at roughly 7ha the largest fort in south-west Scotland); within the interior a number of wooden round-houses provided accommodation for a local community several hundred years before the Romans arrived. By the time the Romans came the defences had fallen into disuse, and it is probable that afterwards the summit was only occupied at intervals.

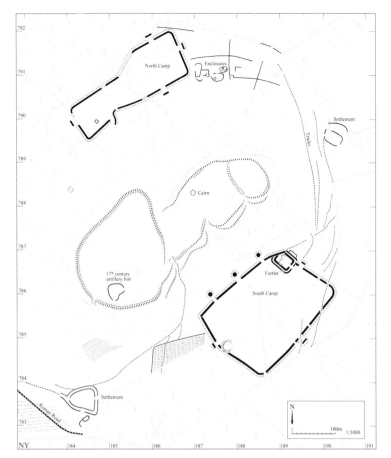

Roman and Native in Conflict

On either side of the large native hillfort of Burnswark lies a Roman temporary camp, the southern example differentiated by the three massive mounds that block its north-west gateways and the long-axis fortlet nestling in its northern angle. The long-abandoned theory that it once marked the scene of a bitter assault may need to be reviewed.

RCAHMS

North Rampart of Burnswark camp

In the languid days of summer legionary units are out on the artillery range at Burnswark Hill, where, in the Antonine period, ballista-firing exercises took place. The heavier weapons occupied massive emplacements at the gateways of a possibly re-used temporary camp, their targets, like those of the cart-mounted catapults, being the dilapidated defences of the abandoned native fortification on the summit.

CHRIS BROWN

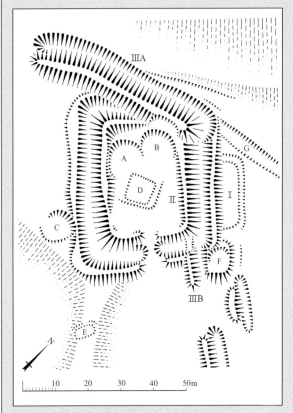

Evidence of Structural Change
This recent detailed survey of the long-axis Antonine fortlet
not only shows how it has been overlain by the north–west
side of the temporary camp, but also hints at the existence
of an even earlier camp.
RCAHMS

The fortlet, defended by a rampart, ditch and
counterscarp bank, was probably built early in the
Antonine period, around AD 140, and may have held
most or all of a century of auxiliary infantry, presumably
one detached from the 1000-strong First Cohort of
Germans at Birrens, 4.5km to the south-east. Why it
differs from all other members of the fortlet group in
lying at such a distance (500m) from the Roman road is
not immediately obvious, as its position has no obvious
tactical advantage. Nevertheless, some time after its
construction, it was incorporated in the northern angle
of a temporary camp of about 5.5ha, one of a pair of
camps, whose partner, about 2.5ha, occupies a similar
position on the opposite side of the hill. The southern
camp might have accommodated a little more than half
a legion – allowing for any specialist equipment required
for its duties here, probably about 3000 men. Under
normal conditions, even if only half the force had

been assigned to camp-building, while the rest stood
guard, each two-man team of diggers and basket-
carriers would have been allocated only 4 feet of the
defence perimeter and the entire circuit could have
been completed in little more than an hour.

The nature of the camp's main purpose is shown
by the three massive mounds built at its entrances on
the side that faces uphill towards the summit and
hillfort. These mounds served as *ballistaria*,
emplacements for the huge artillery pieces of a
Roman legion. From here were fired the stone missiles
that have been found during excavation, scattered in
profusion around the three gateways of the hilltop fort.
Made of local sandstone, and weighing 0.7–1.1kg,
such ballista-balls would have had a deadly effect, but
they formed only part of the lethal barrage, which also
included smaller stone shot (probably fired from lighter,
cart-borne weapons, *carroballistae*), leaden slingshot
and arrows tipped with iron. Since the killing-range of
bow and sling are 140m and 200m respectively, both
could safely have directed fire at the hillfort's gate
from within the camp. Yet the missiles in question
were all targeted at defences that had already
collapsed; in short, they were merely the spent shot
of a field-firing exercise. For a week or two each year,
legionaries would have stayed here under canvas,
improving their skills with torsion-gun, trebuchet, sling
and bow, probably under the supervision of engineers
(*architecti*) seconded for that purpose to nearby
Birrens. The location of the targets they bombarded,
in the dilapidated entrances of the hillfort, would have
had symbolic significance.

So far, the picture is of the pragmatic and
methodical Roman army, practising till it was perfect,
training its troops until the battlefield held fewer
terrors than the parade ground. Yet the story
Burnswark has to tell may be a little less prosaic,
for closer study of its splendidly preserved Roman
remains suggests a more complicated and much more

Ballistic Missiles
Excavation of the hillfort and
training camp at Burnswark
produced many examples of
the stone ballista projectiles
and leaden acorn–shaped
sling–shot which saturated
the target areas at the
hillfort gates.
NATIONAL MUSEUMS
OF SCOTLAND

dramatic history. Detailed examination of the evidence on the ground may indicate that the camp was used on two separate periods, and only in the second was it used for artillery firing practice. The oddly sited fortlet would thus have been built in the north-east angle of an earlier camp, the advantage of re-using the earlier defences outweighing the disadvantage of the site's greater distance from the road. The presumed early Antonine date of the fortlet, together with the camp's 'un-Antonine' lack of regularity, makes it very likely that the latter dates to a much earlier campaign. Moreover, if all three *ballistaria* occupy original gateways, then the first phase camp can be most closely compared with a series of multiple-gated, irregularly-shaped camps in northern England. Being also equivalent in average area to the *combined* areas of the north and south

camps at Burnswark, the English sites, attributed to the campaigns of Petillius Cerealis in AD 71-74, provide a perfect match. IIf that analysis is correct, Burnswark may be the first site in Scotland at which we can identify a scene of military activity preceding that of Agricola, a temporary base of the army of Petillius Cerialis campaigning against some northern part of the Brigantes.

Casting a Long Shadow
The deep shadows of a late summer evening pick out the structural complexities of the artillery training camp at Burnswark, notably the reconstructed north-west side with its three massive ballista–platforms and the inset fortlet.
RCAHMS

Epilogue

It is now AD 411. Magnus Maximus is dead. Although initially successful, having disposed of Gratian, won control of Gaul, Germany, and Spain, and driven Valentinian II out of Italy, in AD 388 he had been drawn into battle with the forces of Theodosius the Great near Aquileia, at the head of the Adriatic. Maximus was defeated, captured, and executed. Seven years later when Theodosius died, the Empire was divided between his two sons, Arcadius and Honorius, under the tutelage of the Vandal generalissimo Count Stilicho; almost immediately the peace was shattered by a rising of Gothic mercenaries led by Alaric, who went on to sack Rome in AD 410. Britain, meanwhile, though rescued from Pictish harassment by Stilicho, had become dissatisfied with the level of support from central government and seen no fewer than three usurpers claim independence from Rome – the latest of these was Constantine III. Constantine, accompanied by the aged Justinianus, now a senior general, had taken an expeditionary force across the Channel to the continent in AD 407, partly to head off a Germanic invasion, and partly to establish an independent western empire of his own. However, in Gaul his luck is running out – one of his lieutenants, Gerontius (Geraint) has taken over a large part of the army and left Constantine under siege in the provincial capital of Arles. His former supporters in Britain have disowned him, seeking – unsuccessfully – to re-align themselves with Honorius. Loyally awaiting the end with his master, the aged Justinianus begins to write a letter to the daughter of his old friend, Magnus Maximus. . .

Execution of Maximus
'A dawn appointment with the headsman, three miles outside Aquileia.'
CHRIS BROWN

JUSTINIANUS COMES, SEVERAE MARCELLINAE SUAE, MAGNI MAXIMI AUGUSTI FILIAE, SALUTEM

scr. Coloniae Juliae Paternae
Sextanorum, Id. Mart., Constantino A. I. et Ignoto conss.

Rogabis forsitan qua re nunc demum scribam. . .

To Severa Marcellina, daughter of the Emperor Magnus
Maximus, Count Justinianus sends his greetings!

> The City of Arles,
> Gallia Viennensis,
> 15th March AD 411

You are probably asking, 'Why does he write now? It's more than
twenty years since Aquileia.' Well, having thrown in my lot with
our new British Constantine, I find myself once more on the
losing side, penned up in Arles together with my imperial master
and about a third of our field army.

Since the end cannot be far off, there are things I must tell
you about your father and the unwritten legacy he bequeathed
to Britannia. In the days when all the West was his, from the
banks of the Rhine to the Pillars of Hercules, he had me join
him on the continent to discuss the worsening situation. He had
clearly foreseen the dangers that would threaten not only our
provinces in Britannia but also the whole Empire. What use did
it serve to have our armies securely lodged in their fortresses if
they were surrounded by an ever more alien land? How long
can we endure if the armies that defend the state are increasingly
composed of the barbarian warriors who most recently battered
at our gates?

Buried Treasure and the Church
The hoard of late-Roman hack-silver
found in Trapain Law hillfort, East
Lothian, included a flagon (right)
depicting the infant Christ and Magi
as well as a spoon (left) with the
Chi-Rho symbol.
NATIONAL MUSEUMS OF SCOTLAND

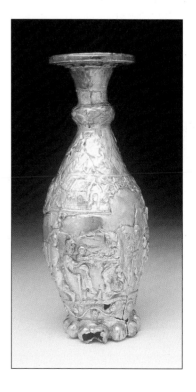

A Legionary Emblem

A carving of the winged horse Pegasus, one of the badges of the Second Augustan Legion, built into a souterrain at Crichton, Midlothian, and probably quarried from a nearby roadside monument after the Romans had evacuated Scotland in the later second century.

RCAHMS

An Empire in Ruins

Aerial photograph of the ruined bath-house at Elginhaugh on the North Esk, revealed by pale-toned parchmarks in pasture. The separate rooms of the rectangular suite are clearly visible, from the cheeks of the stokehole outside the hot room (bottom left) to the frigidarium at the opposite end.

RCAHMS

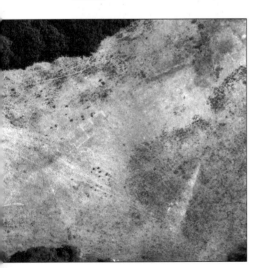

Your father saw that it didn't have to be like that. 'The commanders on the frontier have a duty of care,' he used to say, 'and those in their charge should expect that care to be exercised prudently'. In Britannia, he sought to reduce the military burden by cultivating harmonious links between the people and the administration, on both sides of the frontier. 'The Picts are not the real trouble,' he would say; 'like a wasps' nest, quite harmless till meddled with'. The problem, as he saw it, was to stop the *other* northern tribes becoming too meddlesome; if the Picts were half as bad as folk painted them (and the pun was his), their southern marches would lie closer to York than they do!

In consequence, before he took the troops across to Gaul, he made it his business to develop a real community of interest on the periphery of the outer provinces, not just Britons with Romans, but Britons with Britons. And the people he worked hardest to persuade were the rural magnates of the west and north: he was very successful with the rulers of the tribes beyond the Wall, especially the Damnonii and Novantae, who were already Romanised to the extent of adopting Roman names (partly a result of their conversion to the Christian faith). These were the sorts of people your father would single out for close attention. Of course, it helped enormously that, being a convert to Christianity, he could also claim the kinship of faith – kinship being so important to them.

However, as we knew, what could not be secured by prayer had to be procured by politics. And so we also bound the frontier peoples by solemn oaths and treaties, not just to Rome, but to each other. In theory, this means that if one sector suffers external attack, another will come to its aid, but, in practice, since most neighbouring groups are perennially at each others' throats, it will be a more distant sector (one probably not affected by the same threat) that brings assistance. Thus, if the Ordovices were attacked by the Scotti, it wouldn't be the Brigantes who responded but one of the more northerly tribes, and vice versa.

I'm glad that the arrangements made by Magnus in Britannia have so far proved successful, as I saw at first hand on my last tour of inspection north of the Wall. Apart from opportunistic raids,

the Picts have been discouraged from southward expansion, and the Scotti no longer find the Demetae on the coast of Wales such an attractive target. It's the seaborne threat from the Saxon east which has proved most dangerous, all the more so in the absence of the Expeditionary Force on the Continent. Heaven knows where that leaves us: a disinherited usurper with his army in Gaul, and Britannia defenceless in the face of Saxon assaults.

In short, I have the gravest misgivings. I know what weakness and divided loyalties can do to a country. You haven't seen, as I have, the grass growing rankly on the silent upland stretches of the Eagles' road that once linked the garrisons of the Wall with the shores of Tay and Forth. Only the wind moves now through the ruins of watch-posts and fortlets, way-stations and strongholds. Here and there local people have moved in to loot or squat, or quarry. At Trimontium [Newstead] it was a settlement of northerners, complete with underground storehouses, but even these are now dilapidated and abandoned; a little further on, their kinsfolk have dismantled a wayside monument built by the Second Legion in the time of the Antonines. A day's march beyond that, where a fort guarded the fords across the North Esk, the unit bath-house is being removed stone by stone, whenever

Abandoned Fort-site
An imaginary view of the abandoned fort of Cramond from the north-west, as its stone-walled defences and internal buildings succumb gradually to quarrying and dilapidation, while local Votadinian tribesmen exploit the opportunities on offer. Despite the absence of explicit archaeological evidence, the physical supersession of the fort's *principia* by the parish kirk is a powerful symbol of continuity.
CHRIS BROWN

Heirs to the Roman Legacy
Among the traces of the rectilinear field-system that once supported the garrison and followers at Inveresk, cropmarks reveal the presence of oblong sunken-floored houses built by Dark Age settlers exploiting the same natural resources.
RCAHMS

there's a need for well-cut masonry. On the other hand, some of the forts for example at Inveresk and Cramond have been given a new, and not inappropriate, lease of life as the focus for local native communities, reoccupying the lands that were theirs before the Romans came. At Inveresk, the fort stood guard over some of the richest land in the north, and the fields that once surrounded it are once more vigorously productive.

At Cramond, on the other hand, the ground is generally fertile, but the presence of a tenacious clay makes it hard to work. The main attractions there are the protection afforded by the old fort's curtain-wall and the quarrying resource so readily available, for, unusually in this part of the frontier, the defences and internal buildings were of stone. Another point in its favour is its still-usable harbour (although this must be the only quayside in the Empire where you tie your mooring-line to a lion's-head bollard – a tombstone intended for the fort's graveyard which never quite made it from ship to shore!) More significantly at both Isca and Ambona there are active Christian communities; indeed, at Ambona they meet for worship in the remains of the head-quarters building, which would of course make an excellent church!

Thinking, too, of where the current crisis in Britannia may lead, I ask myself: would it all have been different if Aquileia had gone the other way? What kind of legacy would the 'emperor' Magnus then have bequeathed? Success would have taken him to Rome, or perhaps even to Constantinople, and victors do not

necessarily leave richer legacies than victims. Yet, without a
doubt, your father has an enduring memorial, for he had a
dream: a dream of Empire. And by some miracle, in Britannia he
passed on his vision of what might yet come to pass, not just to
those already in power, but to the hill people of the north and
west, furnishing their minds with a memory of *Romanitas* that
will never be totally erased.

Emblem of Mortality
The stone image of a lioness recently
recovered from the foreshore at
Cramond was probably destined to
ennoble a grave in the cemetery
attached to the fort. A symbol of sudden
death, like other funerary emblems, the
carving also represented the survival of
the soul – a doubly appropriate token
for such a striking pointer to our
Roman heritage.
NATIONAL MUSEUMS OF SCOTLAND

As for the immediate future, however, I see no grounds for hope. Armies and emperors will come and go, and the people will be the poorer. But eventually, someone with power, vision, and luck will shepherd each province, diocese, and prefecture back into the one Western fold. He may not be a Roman – more likely an Ostrogoth or a Frank – but to succeed he must be another Magnus, and his legions will be seen as restoring the Light of Rome!

But enough of prophecy, for it is almost daybreak, and the runner has come who shall, God willing, sneak this letter through the siege-lines.

Farewell.

Birrens Altar Stone

Roman altar dedicated to *Disciplina Augusti* by Antonine troops at Birrens, Dumfries and Galloway. The dedication links two ideas: obedience to the Emperor and military efficiency – doubly appropriate for a garrison stationed near the field-training school at Burnswark.

NATIONAL MUSEUMS OF SCOTLAND

Shortly after this letter was written, Arles fell to the armies of Honorius, and Constantine was executed; of Geraint and Justinianus nothing more is heard. Britain, though now stripped of an imperial defence force, in the sense that the troops that now remained were no longer paid by central government, still considered itself 'Roman', not least because it was still part of the universal Christian Church. Nor was this a one-way view. In AD 429 the bishops of Auxerre and Troyes visited the south of Britain to rescue the British church from the clutches of heresy, and one of them, St Germanus, returning in AD 446-7, became a temporary resistance leader against an invasion of Saxons and Picts. It is possible that this moral support was supplied in lieu of the military aid allegedly sought about this time from Aetius, the Empire's supreme commander in Gaul, by the leaders of the southern communities; such a request (which the roughly contemporary historian Gildas called 'The Groans of the Britons') would not have been thought outrageous by an administration whose hopes of recovering Britain had allowed lists of her long-disbanded garrison to remain on imperial files. Unfortunately, the southern communities in question were already divided by factional strife: Vortigern, traditionally identified as both the son-in-law of Magnus Maximus and the person responsible for inviting Saxon mercenaries into Britain, was at feud with Ambrosius Aurelianus (whose family may also have claimed imperial descent). The stage was thus set for Romano-British society to disintegrate into a maze of warring minor states, gradually overwhelmed by external foes. Despite this, throughout southern and western Britain there lingered memories of a Roman past which were nurtured by something more than just the presence of Christian believers and the existence of trade-links with the Late Roman world. Among these memories, the role played by Magnus Maximus is curiously prominent, especially among the traditions of the British tribes of Wales (in whose eyes he achieved heroic status

Sub-Roman Scotland

Of the many Latin-inscribed stones associated with Early Christian graves in southern Scotland, one of the most interesting is the Yarrow Stone from Selkirkshire. It commemorates two local Dark Age chieftains, Nudos and Dumnogenos. Its reference to them as the 'most renowned princes' (*insignissimi principes*) echoes not only Church Latin, but also the grandiloquent titles of the Late Empire and perhaps Byzantium.
RCAHMS

as Macsen Wledig). But even in Scotland traces of his influence may have lingered – whether in the belief that the royal house of Strathclyde was descended from Maximus, or in the alleged resettlement of Votadini from around Stirling to west Wales, as a defence against marauding Scots. Elsewhere to the north of the Wall there is little concrete evidence of Roman influence beyond what may be attributed to the activity of the early Christian church. On the other hand, that northern church sprang from a Roman model rooted in the late fourth-century province, and who is to say that its survival long after the legions had departed, is not as valid a token of Maximus' achievements on the frontier as any dynastic legacy?

TIMELINE

Year AD	Event	Emperor
43	Invasion of Britain	Claudius
60-61	Revolt of Boudica	Nero
71-74	Petillius Cerealis governor, campaigns in N. England	Vespasian
74-77	Julius Frontinus governor, campaigns in Wales	Vespasian
77-83	Julius Agricola governor, Scottish campaigns	Vespasian, Titus and Domitian
86-87	Northern conquests given up	Domitian
100-105	Retreat to Tyne-Solway	Nerva and Trajan
122	Hadrian's Wall begun	Hadrian
142-144	Antonine Wall built	Antonius Pius
c. 158	?Re-organisation of frontier	Antonius Pius
c. 163-168	?Antonine Scotland given up	Marcus Aurelius
c. 180-184	Hadrian's Wall attacked	Commodus
197	Govern Albinus makes bid for imperial throne and Wall assailed by northern tribes	Pertinax, Julianus and Severus
208-211	Septimius Severus campaigns against Maeatae and Caledonii dies at York	Septimius Severus
212-215	Caracalla abandons northern outposts in Scotland	Caracalla
287-296	Carausius unsurps power	Constantius Chlorus
305-306	Constantius Chlorus campaigns against Caledonians 'and other Picts' and dies at York	Constantius Chlorus
c. 315	?Successful campaign against Picts	Constantine I
343	?Pictish unrest	Constans
360	Scots and Picts attack frontier areas	Constantius II
364-369	Picts (comprising Verturions and Dicalydones) rebuffed by Count Theodosius	Valentinian I
382-383	Invading Picts and Scots defeated by Magnus Maximus, who usurps power	Theodosius I
396-398	Pictish attack countered by Stilicho	Honorius
407	British usurper Constantine III siezes power	Honorius
409-410	Britain rejects Constantine III and is given control of its own affairs	Honorius
429-446	Last links and appeals for help	Valentinian III

'Roman Scotland' (marked spanning 71 to 212-215)

Flavian (marked spanning 71-74 to 86-87)

How Do I Find Out More?

Sites To Visit

Visible traces of Roman military structures are to be found in many parts of Scotland south of the Grampians. Unfortunately, it is not always the most important sites that are best preserved, nor are these a wholly representative sample of the various defence systems of which they once formed part. Furthermore, most having been built in such impermanent materials as turf and timber, and rarely of stone, their remains often seem difficult to appreciate on the ground, and even when excavated cannot be presented to the visitor with the structural impact of, say, a chambered tomb or a stone circle. Nevertheless, their regular plan and the knowledge that we possess about their function often help us to see them more clearly in meaningful relationship to an ancient landscape, especially in the case of the larger monuments, like roads and temporary camps, which may even bulk large in the modern countryside.

A number of the sites listed below are opened to the public by Historic Scotland (HS) or other agencies (P), but many are in private ownership and permission should be sought from the owner before making a visit; due care should of course be taken, to avoid both damage to the monument and any personal injury arising from, for example, rough or uneven ground. The sites are grouped alphabetically in local authority areas, with Ordnance Survey grid references indicating their location.

Aberdeenshire

Durno – very large marching-camp (58ha), probably used by the army of Agricola on its way to the battle of *Mons Graupius* in AD 83; no traces of the camp above ground, but the view from within it, looking south towards 528m-high Bennachie (thought by some to be *Graupius* itself), embraces a magnificent possible battlefield.
NJ 699272.

Raedykes – 38ha marching-camp, probably Agricolan, its very irregular defence-circuit is visible on the ground for much of the perimeter.
NO 841902.

Borders

Brownhart Law – fortlet guarding upland sector of Roman road Dere Street, midway on a highly walkable route from Pennymuir (q.v.) across the Border to the complex of Roman works at Chew Green in England.
NT 790096.

Channelkirk – very large and irregularly shaped Severan marching-camp (65ha), adjoining Roman road Dere Street at south end of particularly well-preserved upland sector of several km.
NT 473548.

Eildon Hill – very large (16ha) prehistoric hillfort occupying the northernmost of the three-peaked Eildon Hills; on the summit, surrounded by the scooped platforms of Iron Age timber houses, there is the penannular ditch of a Roman signal-station.
NT 554328.

Lyne – the visible earthworks of an Antonine fort occupy a prominent position in a bend of the Lyne Water; invisible nearby lie the remains of temporary camps and a fortlet, as well as, on the opposite bank, the Flavian fort of Easter Happrew.
NT187405.

Newstead – situated in a classic bridgehead position on the south bank of the Tweed, and at the foot of the imposing Eildon massif, the superimposed remains of at least four forts and their annexes, together with several hundred hectares occupied by large marching-camps of all periods; few visible traces, but as evidence of Roman 'eye' for ground, an unsurpassed location.
NT 571343.

Pennymuir – beside the Roman road Dere Street lie the superimposed remains of two marching-camps, the defence-perimeter of both surviving almost intact; the truncated traces of two more can be made out in pasture to the east. Immediately to the south rises Woden Law, where a native hillfort is enclosed within earthworks once thought to be Roman siege-lines.
NT755140.

Central Scotland
Bar Hill – fort on the Antonine Wall, but detached from the barrier; internal buildings of stone (headquarters, bath-house and latrine); adjacent stretch of the Wall itself, bypassing prehistoric hillfort (HS).
NS 707759.

Bearsden – bathhouse suite of Antonine Wall fort consolidated after excavation (HS).
NS545720.

Braidwood to Carlops – fine upland stretch of Roman road with occasional quarry-pits.
NT 165565 to 192592.

Castle Greg – surprisingly well-preserved early Flavian fortlet, unassociated with road-system and displaying parrot's-beak ditch terminals (P).
NT 050592.

Cramond – site of coastal fort and large extramural settlement of Antonine and Severan date, now overlain by village of Cramond; some internal buildings (headquarters, granary and workshops) consolidated after excavation (P).
NT 189768.

Croy Hill – magnificent upland stretch of the Antonine Wall, the ditch here being rock-cut, and including the sites of a Wall-fort (and fortlet), as well as possible beacon-platforms (HS).
NS 722762 to 741770.

Inveresk — site of coastal cavalry fort and large extramural settlement of Antonine date, now overlain respectively by churchyard and modern Inveresk; remains of hypocausted building in adjacent private garden.
NT 342720.

Kinneil – site of Antonine Wall-fortlet excavated and consolidated (P), with adjacent traces of the barrier overlooking the estuarine waters of the Forth.
NS 977803.

Rough Castle – very well preserved defensive perimeter of Antonine Wall fort (including the famous 'lily-bed' man-traps), with nearby beacon-platforms and magnificent adjoining sectors of the barrier itself (the ditch and counterscarp bank being especially impressive)(HS).
NS 834798 to 856798.

Seabegs Wood – well preserved stretch of the Antonine Wall, the counterscarp bank being particularly remarkable; at the west end the dog-leg change of alignment indicates the presence of a Wall-fortlet (HS&P).
NS 811791 to 815793.

Clydesdale
Bothwellhaugh, Strathclyde Park – Antonine fort and bathhouse, the defences of the former faintly visible, but in a commanding position, the latter excavated and reconstructed (P).
NS 731577.

Cleghorn – marching-camp of c. 18ha and probably Antonine, the north rampart, with two tutulus-guarded gates, preserved in Camp Wood.
NS 910459.

Crawford – small Agricolan and Antonine fort, guarding an important road-junction; its position is indicated by the prominent rectangular platform to the north-west of the medieval motte; the Roman road can be followed for several kilometres to north and south.
NS953214.

Daer to Potrail Water – fine stretch of Roman road leading south-west from Crawford (q.v.), with quarry-pits, stream crossings, and well preserved road-mound; connects with Durisdeer (q.v. Dumfries and Galloway).
NS 915059 to 956163.

Little Clyde – marching-camp of probable Antonine date; sections of rampart and ditch survive (including gate with tutulus), but most significant is the absolute regularity of plan on very awkward terrain.
NS 994159.

Redshaw Burn – Antonine fortlet guarding upland road-sector between Clyde and Annan; road well worth walking, despite enveloping forestry, to connect with White Type watch-tower (q.v. Dumfries and Galloway) on south-east.
NT 030139.

Dumfries and Galloway

Birrens – conspicuous earthworks of large fort occupied in the Flavian, Hadrianic, and Antonine periods. NY 219752.

Burnswark – splendidly preserved and very important complex of structures, adjoining large prehistoric hillfort and comprising temporary camps of various periods as well as long-axis Antonine fortlet, the former holding troops engaged in field-firing exercises. NY 186787.

Drumlanrig – platform of presumed Agricolan and Antonine bridgehead fort above the Nith, conspicuous amidst landscaped policies of major country seat (P). NX 854989.

Durisdeer – well preserved long-axis Antonine fortlet in impressive position guarding upland pass; the Roman road leading from Clydesdale into Nithsdale very well preserved in this sector, connecting with Daer-Potrail Water stretch (q.v. Clydesdale). NX 902048.

Raeburnfoot – small Antonine bridgehead fort enclosed by annexe, the defences of both being exceptionally well-preserved. NY 251990.

White Type – Antonine roadside watch-tower with extensive views from the Devil's Beeftub southward into Annandale; rare example – small, but beautifully preserved. NT 055119 .

Perthshire and Angus

Ardoch – outstandingly important complex, comprising multi-period fort with splendidly preserved defences and annexes, together with several temporary camps of various sizes and dates (P). NN839099.

Black Hill, Meikleour – Flavian watch-tower on isolated hillock guarding north-east approaches to Inchtuthil (q.v.). NO176391.

Fendoch – Flavian glen-blocking fort of earth and timber, its classic site indicated by prominent platform facing the mouth of the Sma Glen, with contemporary watch-tower on high ground 800m to the north-west. NN 919283.

Gask Ridge – series of Flavian watch-towers (some HS) adjoining Roman road between the Earn and the Tay, much of which underlies public highway or forestry track. NN 917185 to NO 020205.

Inchtuthil – Flavian legionary fortress, enclosure and temporary camps, occupying plateau on north bank of the Tay; much of the defence-perimeter of the fortress remains visible in pasture, together with contemporary compound, and superimposed Dark Age burial-mounds. NO125397.

Innerpeffray – in southern fringes of wood, a stretch of the north rampart and ditch of 53ha Severan marching-camp, as well as well-preserved Flavian watch-tower to the north, looking on to westward extension of the Gask Ridge road (q.v.). NN 916184.

Kaims Castle – remains of double-ditched Flavian fortlet with adjacent stretch of Roman causeway, associated with possible Forth-Tay watch-tower system, crowns hillock in loop of modern road north of Ardoch (q.v.). NN 860129.

Kirkbuddo – considerable length of rampart and ditch of 25ha Severan marching-camp. NO 491442.

(above)

Lowland Watch and Ward

At Murder Loch, on the route from
Annandale to lower Nithsdale, a small
roadside post has succumbed to intensive
cultivation, now recognisable only as a
pattern of cropmarks.

RCAHMS

(right)

Dalginross Fort, near Comrie

A classic cropmark representation of a
Roman fort founded in the Agricolan
period and re-occupied in the Antonine.

RCAHMS

Museums

Within the areas identified above, most local authority museums will include displays of Roman material, those at Dumfries, Dundee, Falkirk and Perth being able to draw on a wealth of artefacts from neighbouring sites, while specifically site-related museums, such as Kinneil House and Melrose (for Newstead), are also well worth a visit. Pride of place must go to the Roman collections housed in the new Museum of Scotland, Chambers Street, Edinburgh, and the Hunterian Museum of the University of Glasgow (both of which may be accessed on the Internet). Of further interest is the possibility that the Archaeolink Prehistory Park at Oyne, Aberdeenshire, may soon include among its exhibits a reconstruction of a Roman marching-camp of Stracathro type!

Further Reading

- *Roman Scotland*, David Breeze (Batsford 1996).

- *The Romans in Scotland*, Gordon Maxwell (Mercat Press 1989).

- *Scotland's Roman Remains*, Lawrence Keppie (John Donald 1986).

- *Oxford Illustrated History of Roman Britain*, Peter Salway (Oxford University Press 1993).

- *Roman Britain from the Air*, Sheppard Frere and Kenneth St Joseph (Cambridge University Press 1983).

- *Agricola and the Conquest of the North*, William Hanson (Batsford 1987).

- *A Battle Lost: Romans and Caledonians at Mons Graupius*, Gordon Maxwell (Edinburgh University Press 1990).

- *Rome's North-West Frontier: the Antonine Wall*, William Hanson and Gordon Maxwell (Edinburgh University Press 1983).

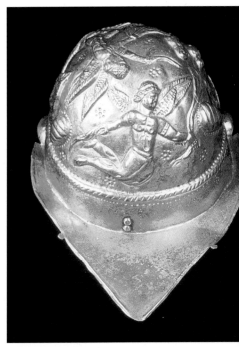

Newstead helmet
An expensive and richly decorated cavalry helmet from Newstead which would not have been exposed to the hazards of the battlefield.
NATIONAL MUSEUMS OF SCOTLAND

Note: Magnus Maximus and Justinianus are real historical figures, though there is no evidence that they were involved jointly in any of the events described in this book. That Vortigern, by tradition a leading figure in fifth-century Britain, was Maximus' son-in-law, is actually recorded on the Pillar of Eliseg, a ninth-century memorial in Powys; the name of Maximus' daughter, however, has been invented. The title of this book refers to Matthew's Gospel, chapter 24, verse 28: 'Wheresoever the carcass is, there will the eagles be gathered together.'

Acknowledgements

I am very grateful to the many friends and colleagues who have helped in the preparation and production of this book: for editorial contributions far beyond the call of duty, to Gordon Barclay and Jackie Henrie; to Hugh Andrew for invaluable advice and encouragement; to Chris Brown and Sylvia Stevenson respectively for the reconstructions and line-drawings that so handsomely amplify the text; to staff of the National Monuments Record Photographic Section, and Drawing Office of the Royal Commission of the Ancient and Historical Monuments of Scotland (RCAHMS), who assembled much of the additional illustrative material, as also to Donald Reid for putting the resultant collection in due order. My thanks are also expressed to the following organisations and individuals for their permission to reproduce specific illustrations: the Royal Commission on the Historical Monuments of England, copyright holder of the illustration on page 17; the Society of Antiquaries of London, copyright holder of the illustrations on pages 19 (top) and 42 (bottom); Lawrence Keppie and the Glasgow Archaeological Society, copyright holder of the illustration on page 44 (bottom right); David Breeze; Angus Lamb; Historic Scotland; the Hunterian Museum, University of Glasgow; National Museums of Scotland; and the RCAHMS.